Whimsical Willies
The Adults-Only Funny & Naughty Cock Coloring Book

By NawteeFun

THIRTY FUN, PHALLIC DESIGNS!

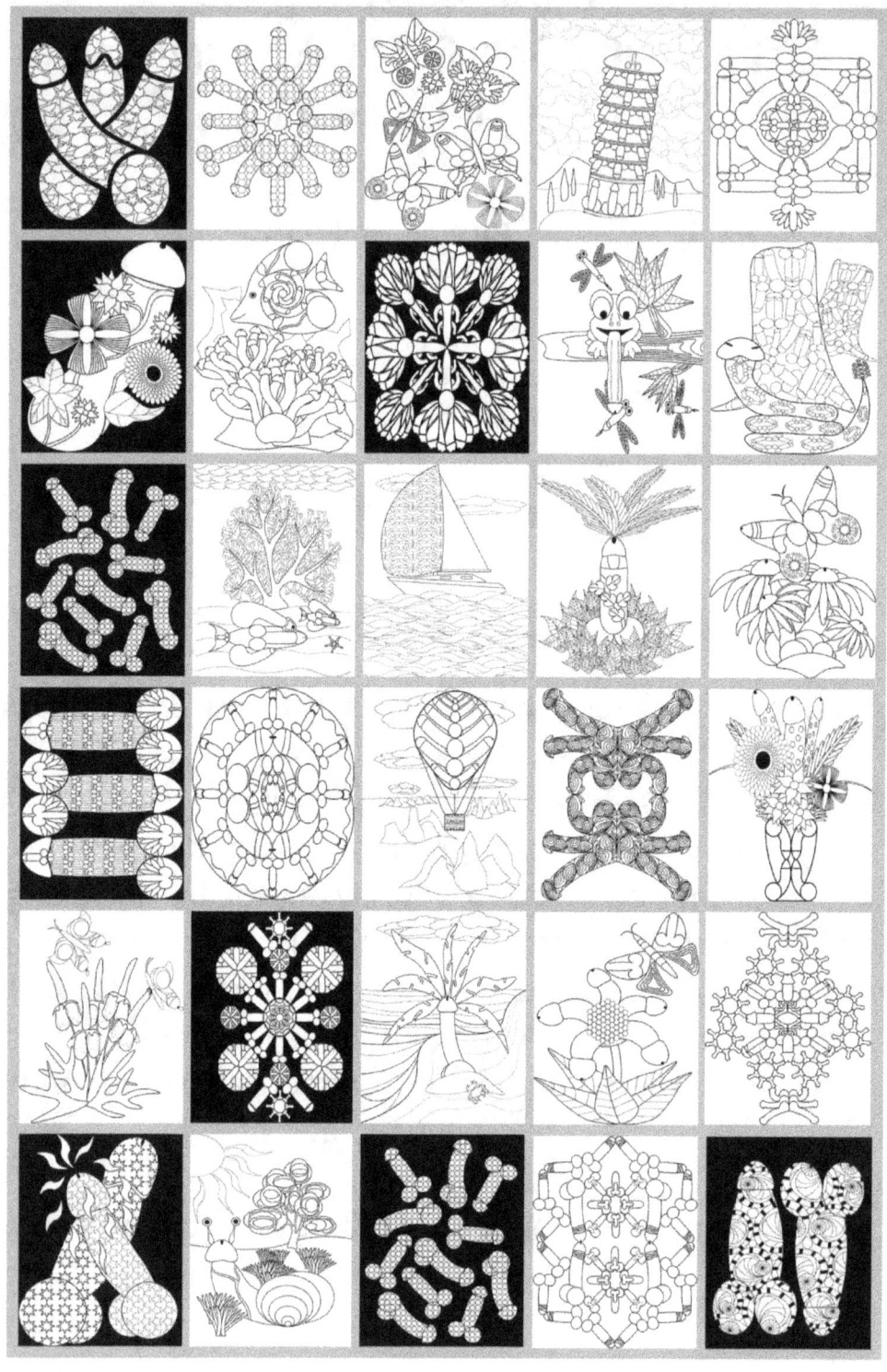

Welcome!

Whimsical Willies: The Adults-Only Funny & Naughty Cock Coloring Book is filled with (soon to be) colorful cocks, dazzling dicks, and a plethora of pulchritudinous penises!

Text pages with cock-themed dirty jokes appear between the coloring pages of this book to provide both some added humor and description of the images, as well as to provide a bleed-through buffer for those using coloring pens.

There are 30 different naughty coloring pages in this book, with a wide variety in theme and design complexity, allowing for adult coloring enjoyment for beginners and experts alike. A mixture of both white and black background coloring images are included. While some may purchase this book simply as a humorous and slightly dirty gag gift or adult party activity (birthday parties, bridal showers, bachelorette/hen parties, etc.), it is intended to provide plenty of fun and entertainment for serious colorists as well.

If you have comments, questions, and/or requests for content in future adult coloring or game books, or if you would like to join our email list to receive notices of new products and exclusive FREE subscriber-only coloring pages and other content, please visit us at:

Nawteefun.com

"God gave men a penis and a brain, but unfortunately not enough blood supply to run both at the same time."

- Robin Williams

The mosaic pattern on a black background allows for a dramatic kaleidoscope of color on the following trio of crossed cocks for your adult coloring pleasure.

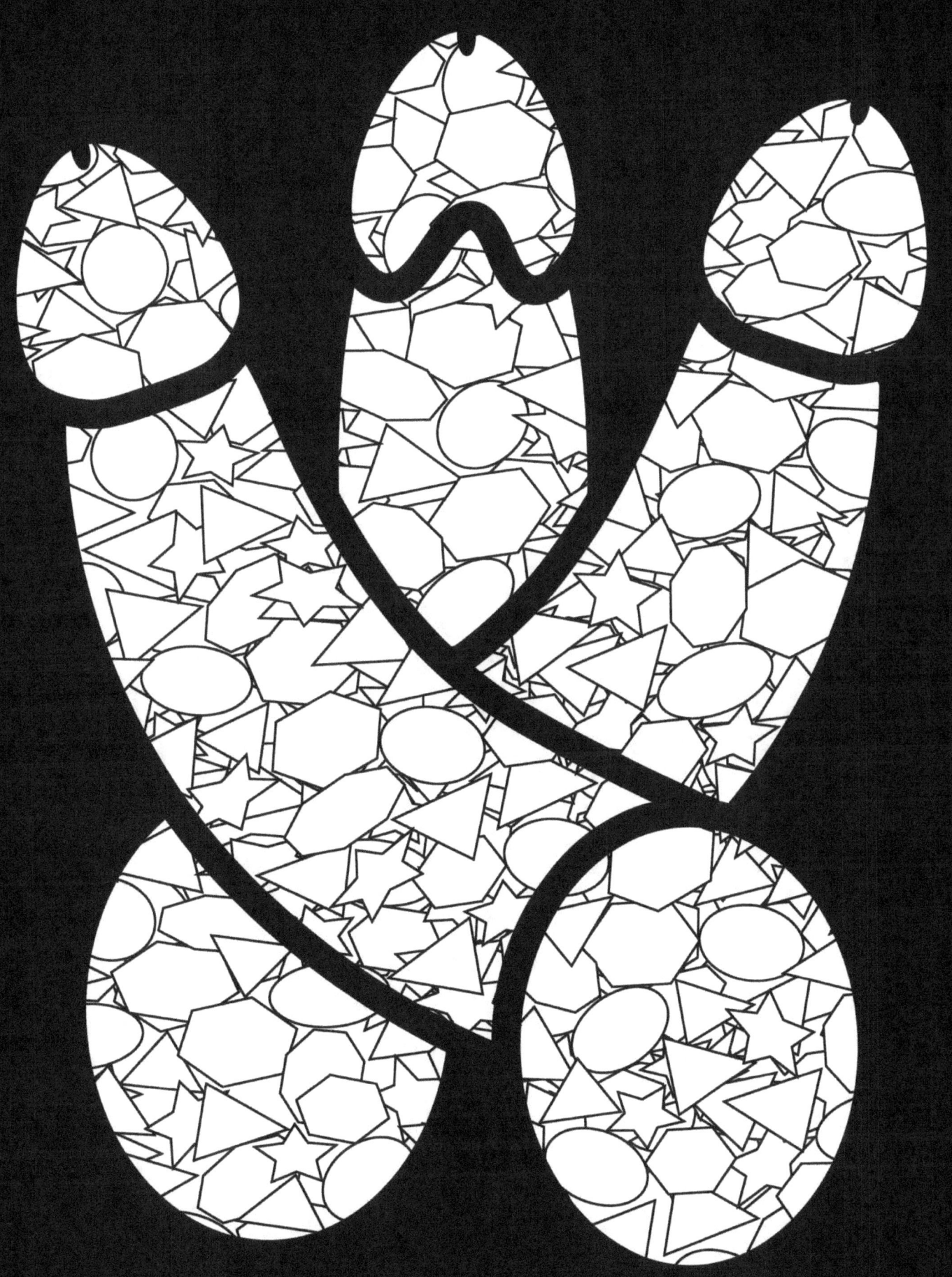

"They say that penis size is related to shoe size. That makes the thought of getting fucked by a clown even scarier!"

- Anonymous

Mandalas are a popular theme for adult coloring books, and on the next page, you'll find a wonderfully cocky one to meditate on!

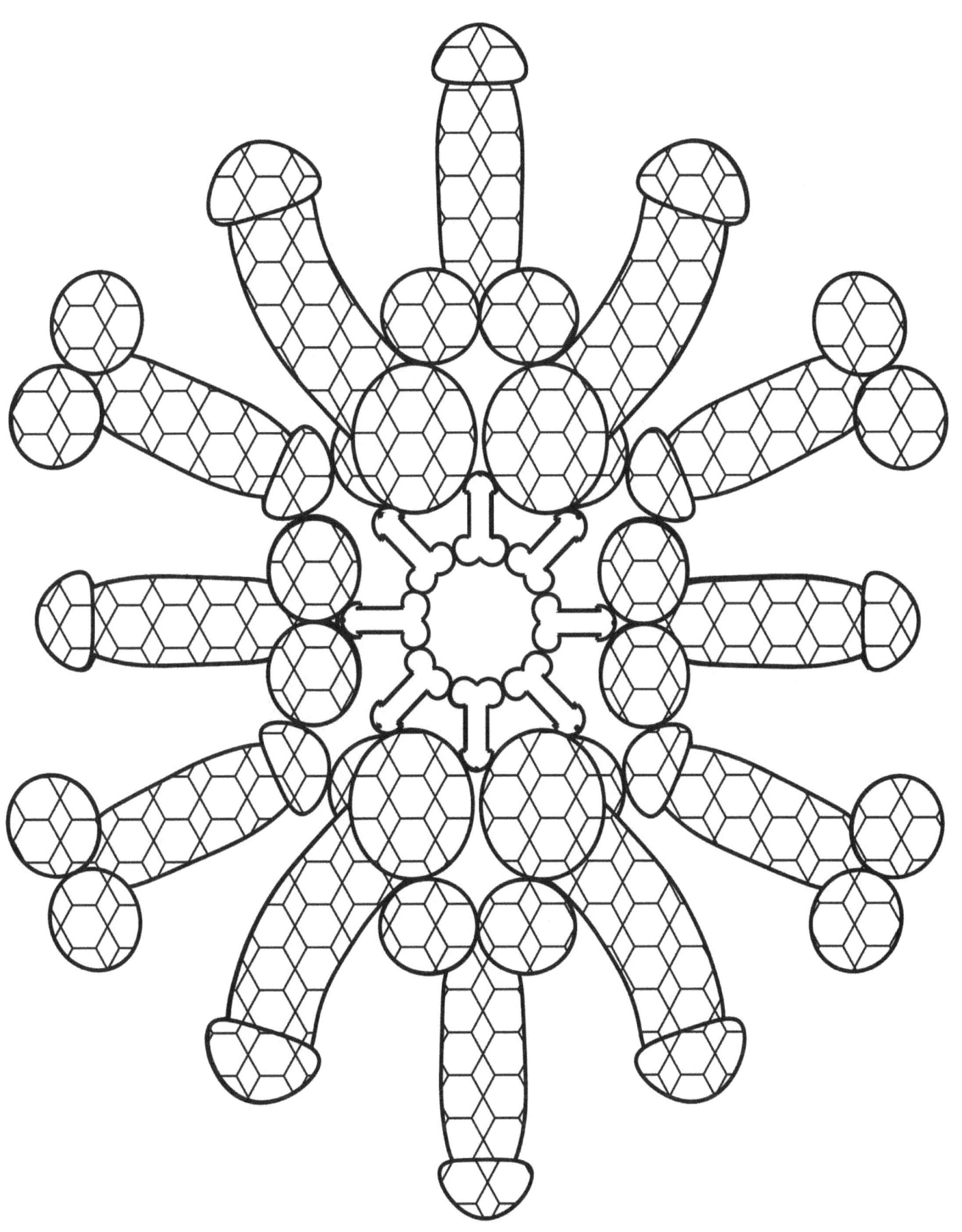

"My new girlfriend tried to reassure me by saying that a small penis shouldn't be an issue in a loving relationship. I still wish she didn't have one!"

- Anonymous

Some people have very dirty minds and see sexual images in the most innocent of things – take the butterflies on the next coloring page for example.

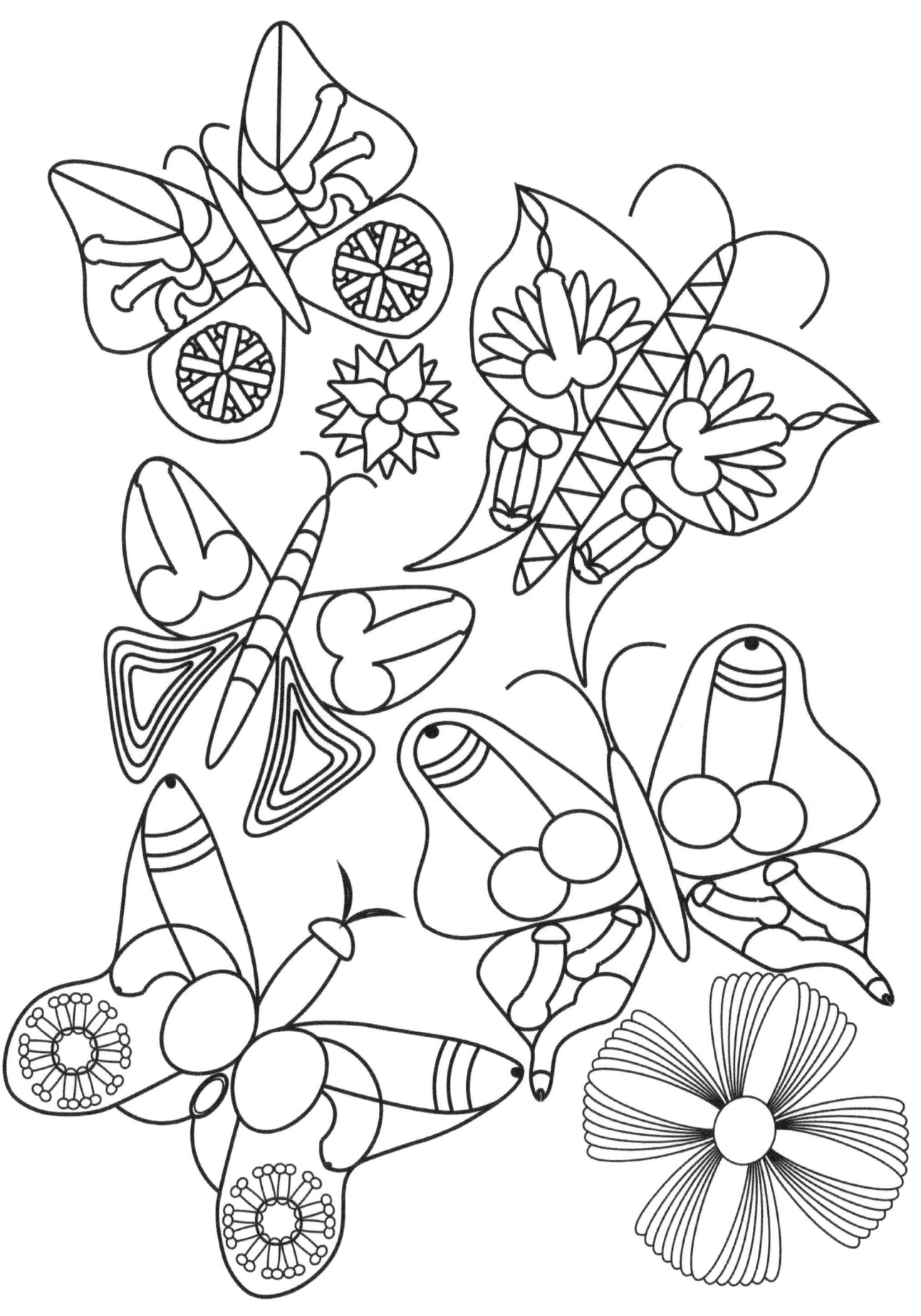

Interesting Facts(?): A man's erect penis is approximately three times the length of his thumb. The femur is the longest bone in the body and is as hard as concrete. On average, women blink twice as often as men do. Over 300 muscles are required to keep our balance when we stand. The strongest muscle in the body for its size is the masseter in the jaw. The vast majority of women will have read this entire text. The vast majority of men are staring at their thumbs.

Looking for some stress-relief? Perhaps you need a vacation to go see some of the world's most exciting places. To get you in the proper mindset, how about a imagining a trip to Italy while coloring the famous Leaning Tower of Penisa?

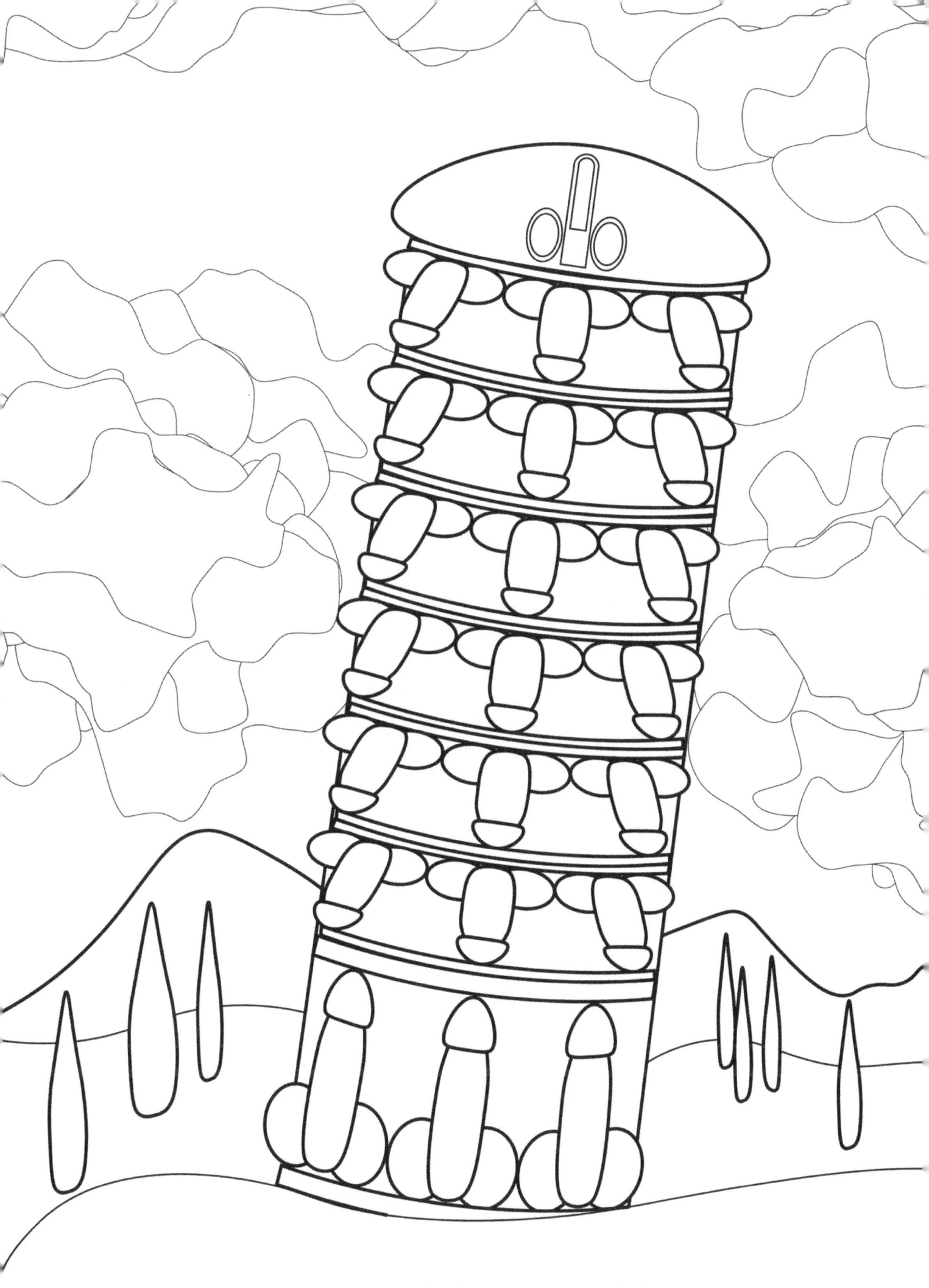

"My mom told me that the secret to pleasing a man is through his stomach. But I have found a convenient detour through the penis."

- Kristen Schaal

The following erotic coloring page was actually inspired by the decorative tiles adorning the walls at a nearby shopping center. They didn't have actual cocks on them, but with only a small amount of dirty imagination, they sure looked like it!

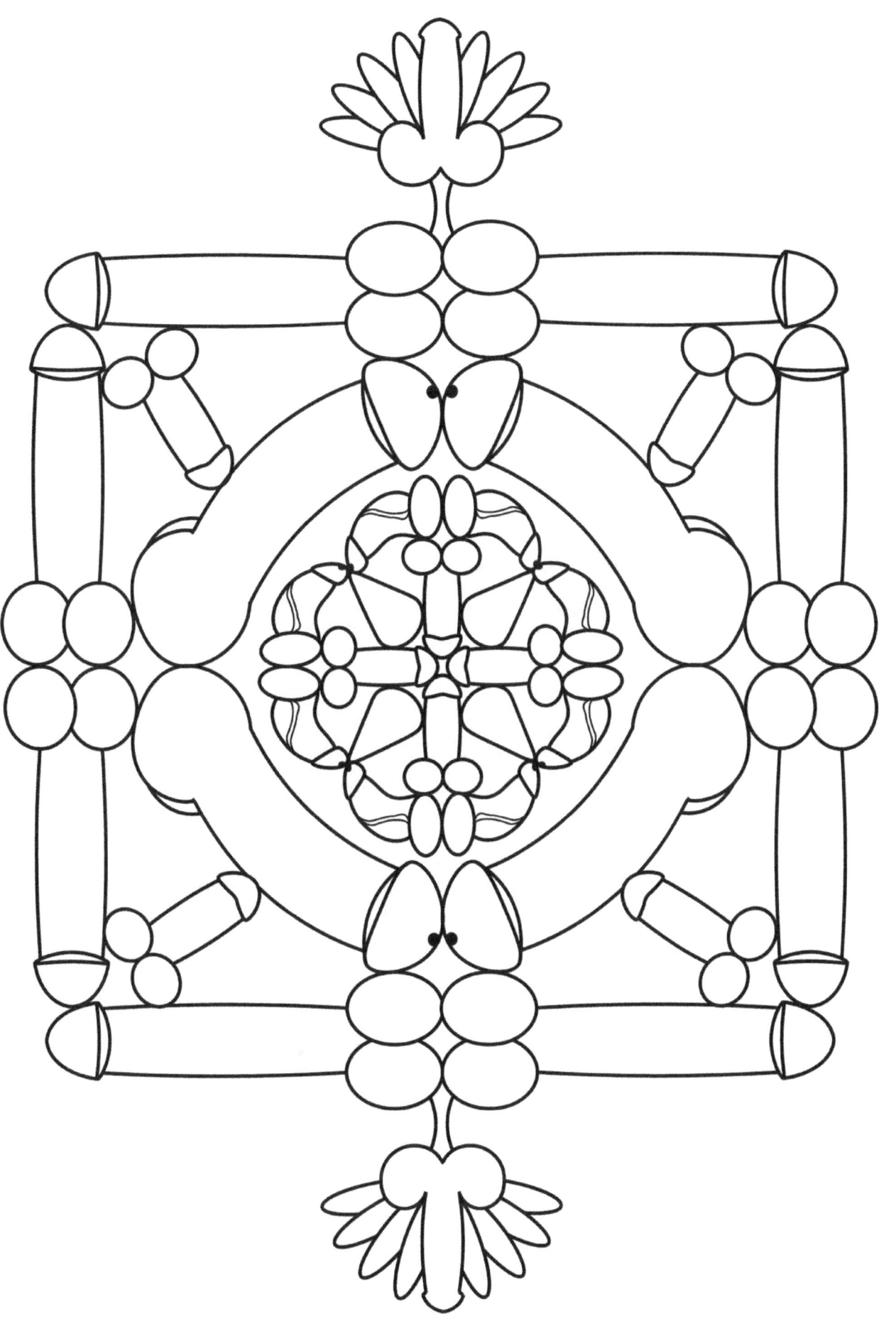

"When 3 people have sex, it's called a threesome. When 2 people have sex, it's called a twosome. I guess that means I'm handsome!"

- Anonymous

Next, we have a big flowering phallus on a black background for your naughty coloring fun!

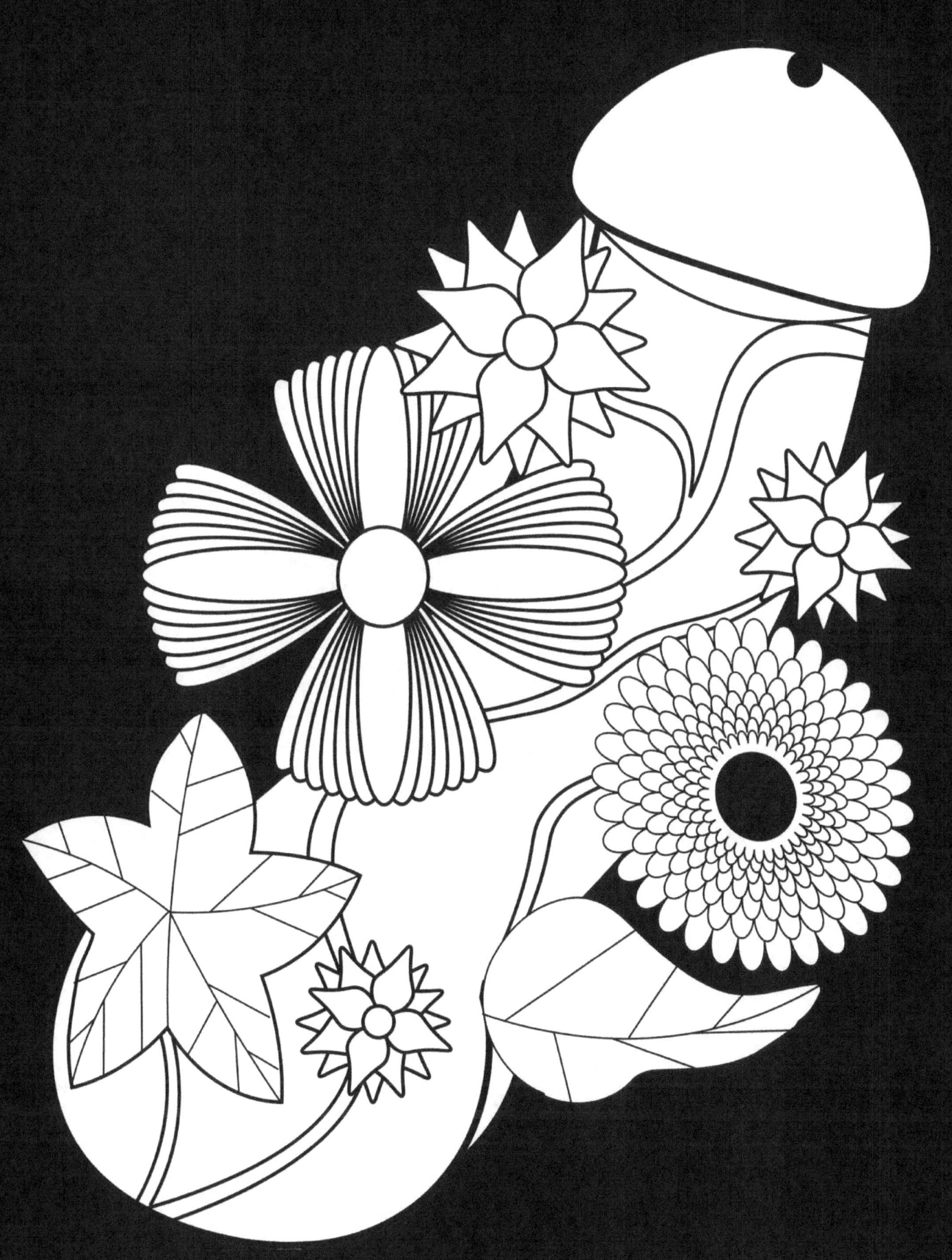

How can you spot the blind guy at the nudist colony? It's not hard.

- Anonymous

Studies have shown that watching fish in an aquarium can help men and women alike with stress-relief and anger management. The same can be said for sex. The next risqué page in our adult coloring book combines a little of both.

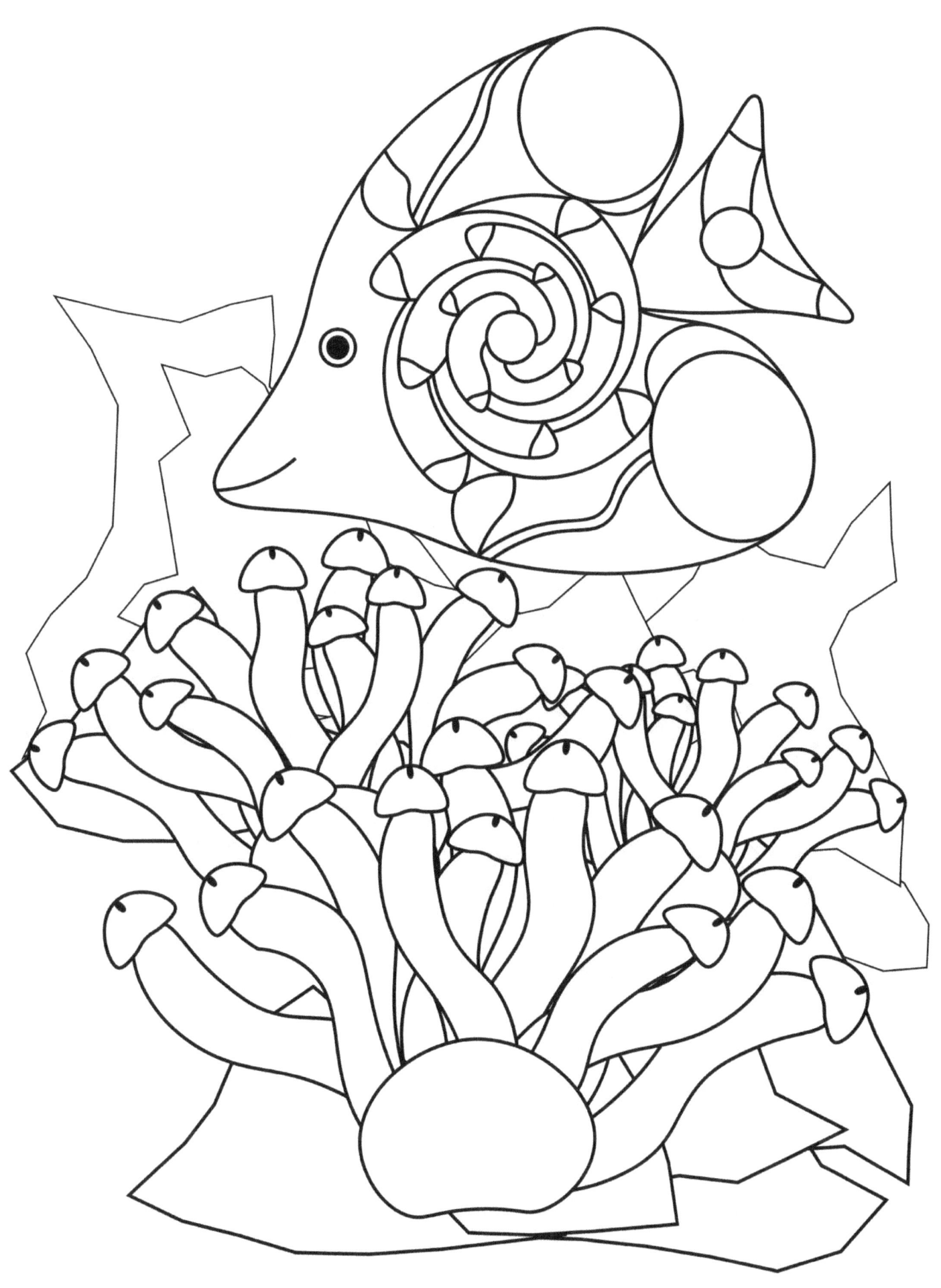

"Those penis enlargement pills are really working for you! You're becoming a bigger dick every day!"

- Anonymous

Time for another MAN-dala! (See what I did there?)
This one has a black background for a dramatic flair.

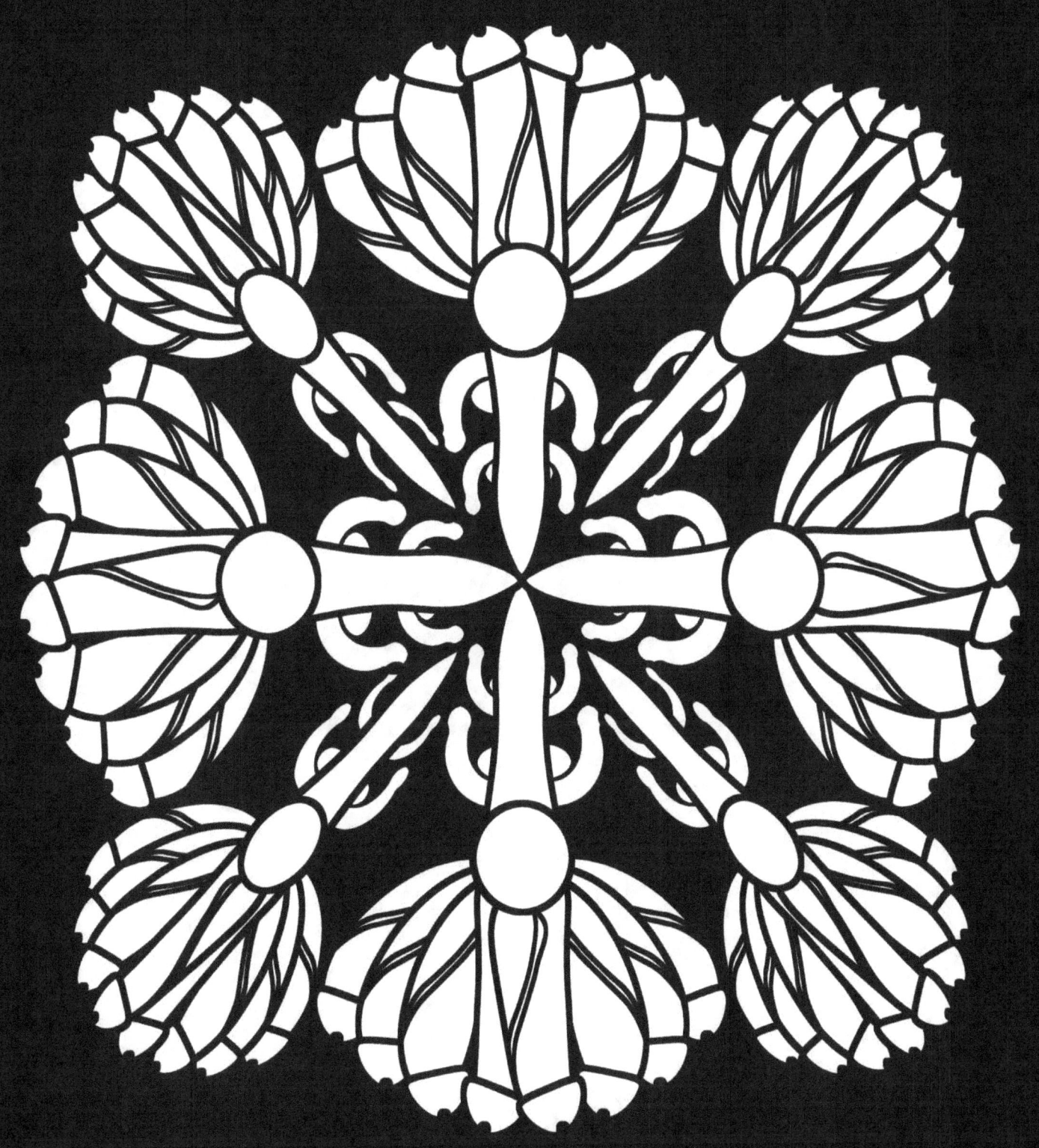

"Son, when you have a tool like mine, you have to build a shed over it!"

- Anonymous Guy With Huge Beer Gut

Speaking of tools, animals sometimes have remarkable tools that give them big advantages for survival. For instance, frogs like the one on the next page of our adult coloring book, have amazing tongues!

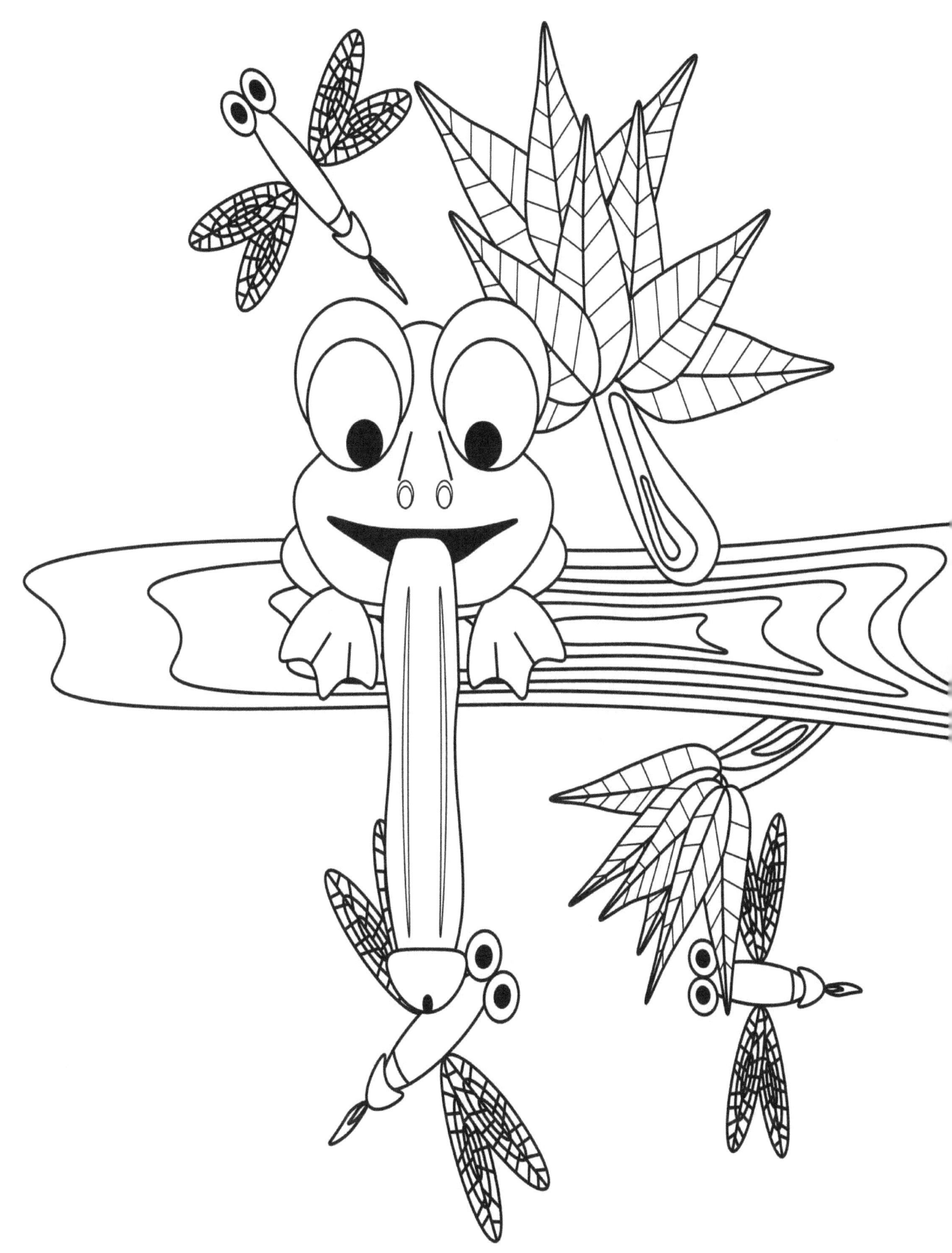

What should you do if you girlfriend starts smoking? Slow down and use a lubricant.

- FAQ of A Sex Doll Owner's Manual

Always beware of the fearsome trouser snake! If you do encounter one, be sure to protect your eyes – they've been known to spit!

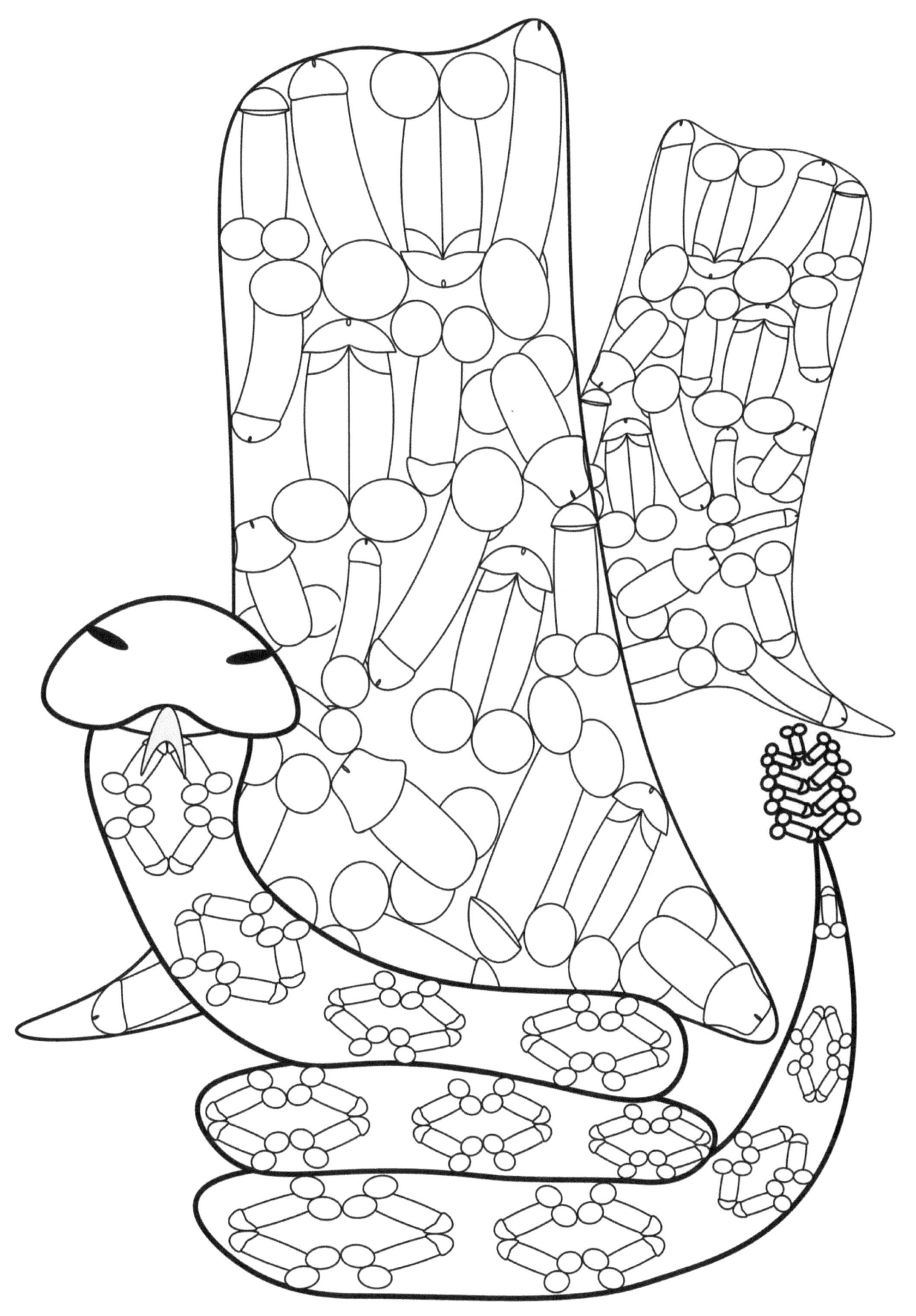

"Wow, those are some gorgeous testicles you have!"

- Nobody – Ever!

They say that all penises look the same in the dark, but they haven't seen this one!

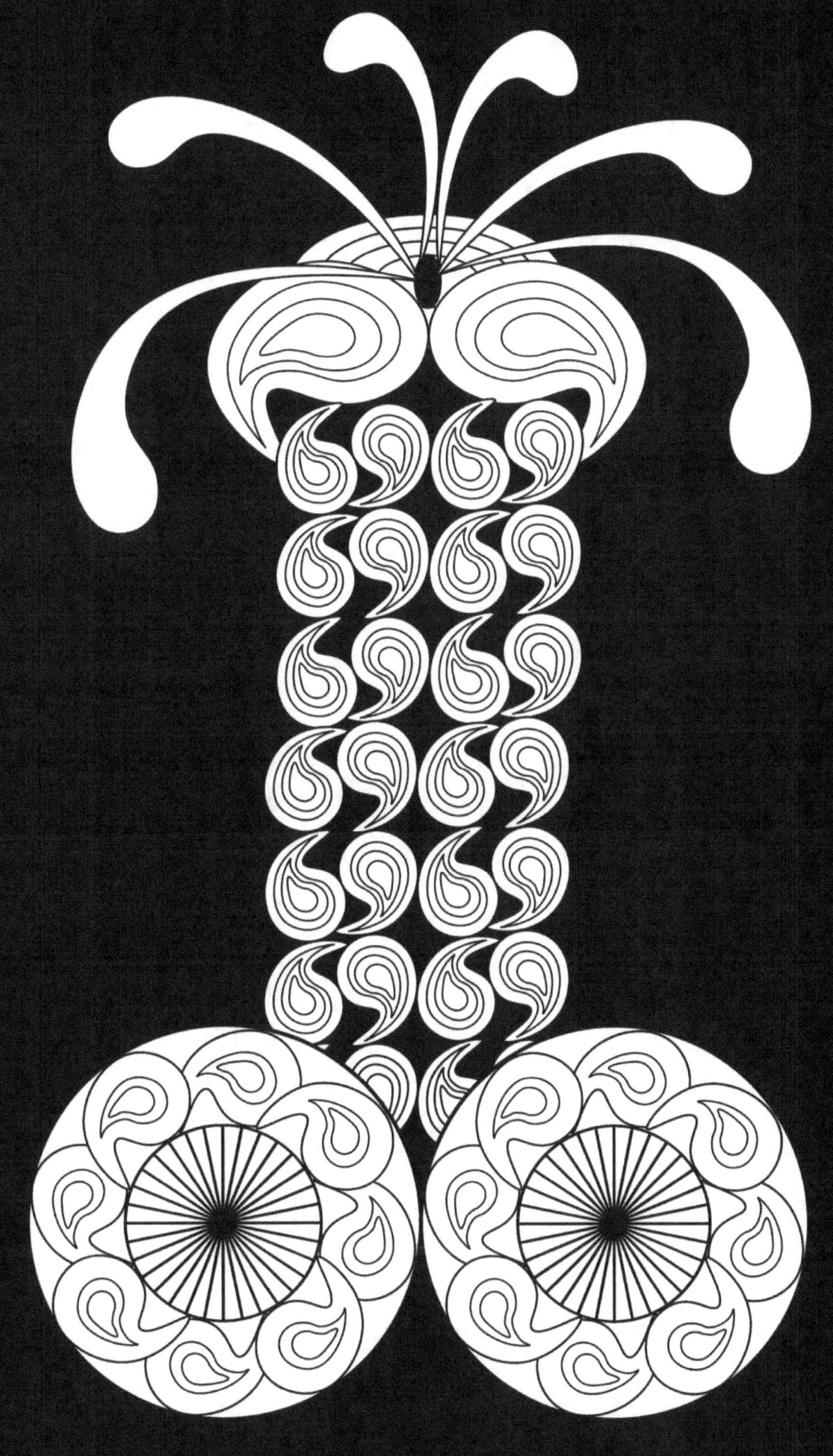

"Give it to me!" she yelled, a ferocious passion rising in her voice. "I'm so wet! Give it to me now!" she begged.

She could scream all she wanted. I was keeping the umbrella.

- Anonymous

Speaking of wet, here's some more phallic fish for your adult coloring pleasure.

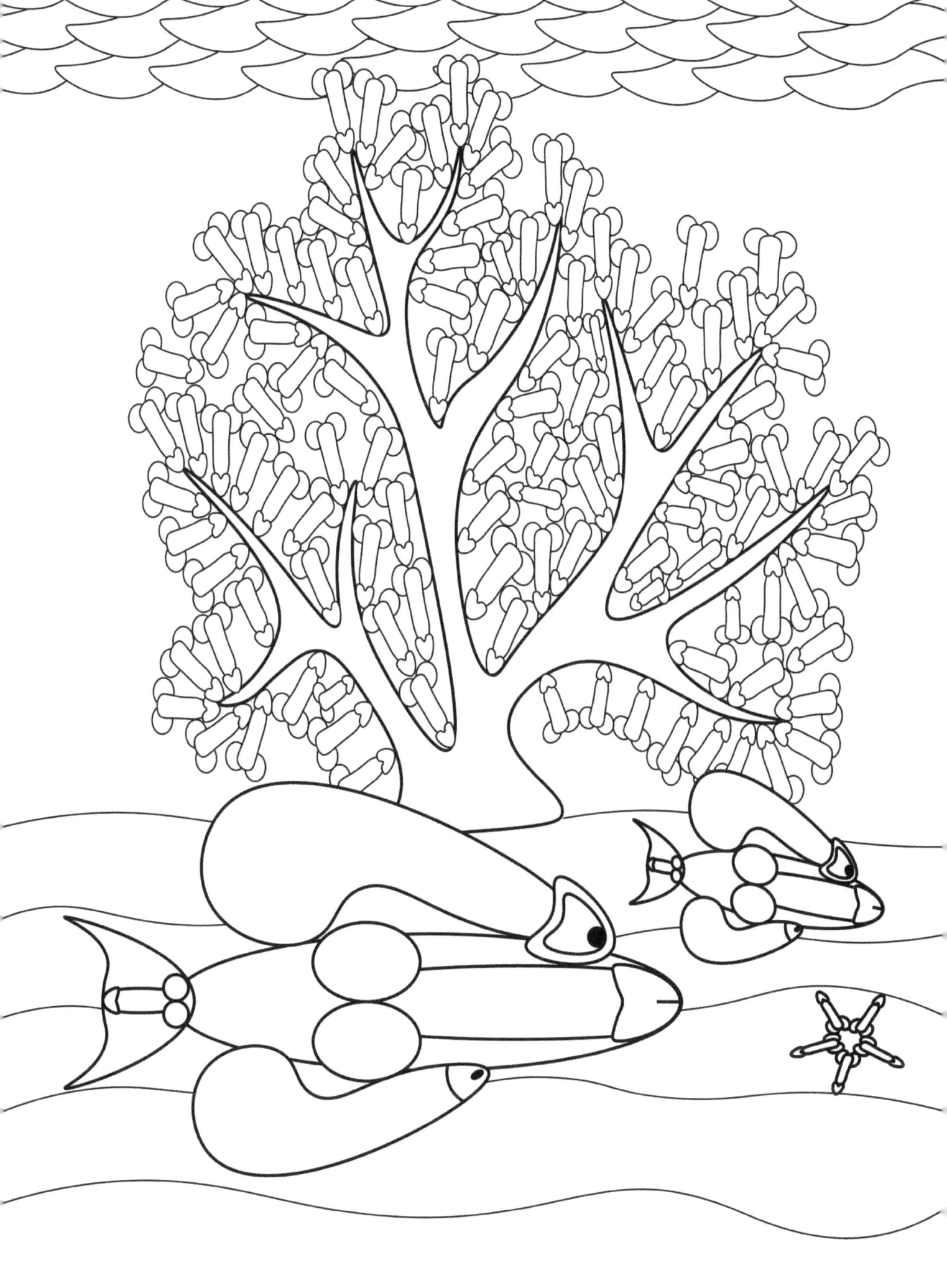

"Hey! Hey! HEY!!!"

- Everyone experiencing butt stuff for the first time without being warned by their partner that he or she was making that move.

While we're on an ocean theme, there's a relaxing picture of a slightly naughty sailboat on the next page.

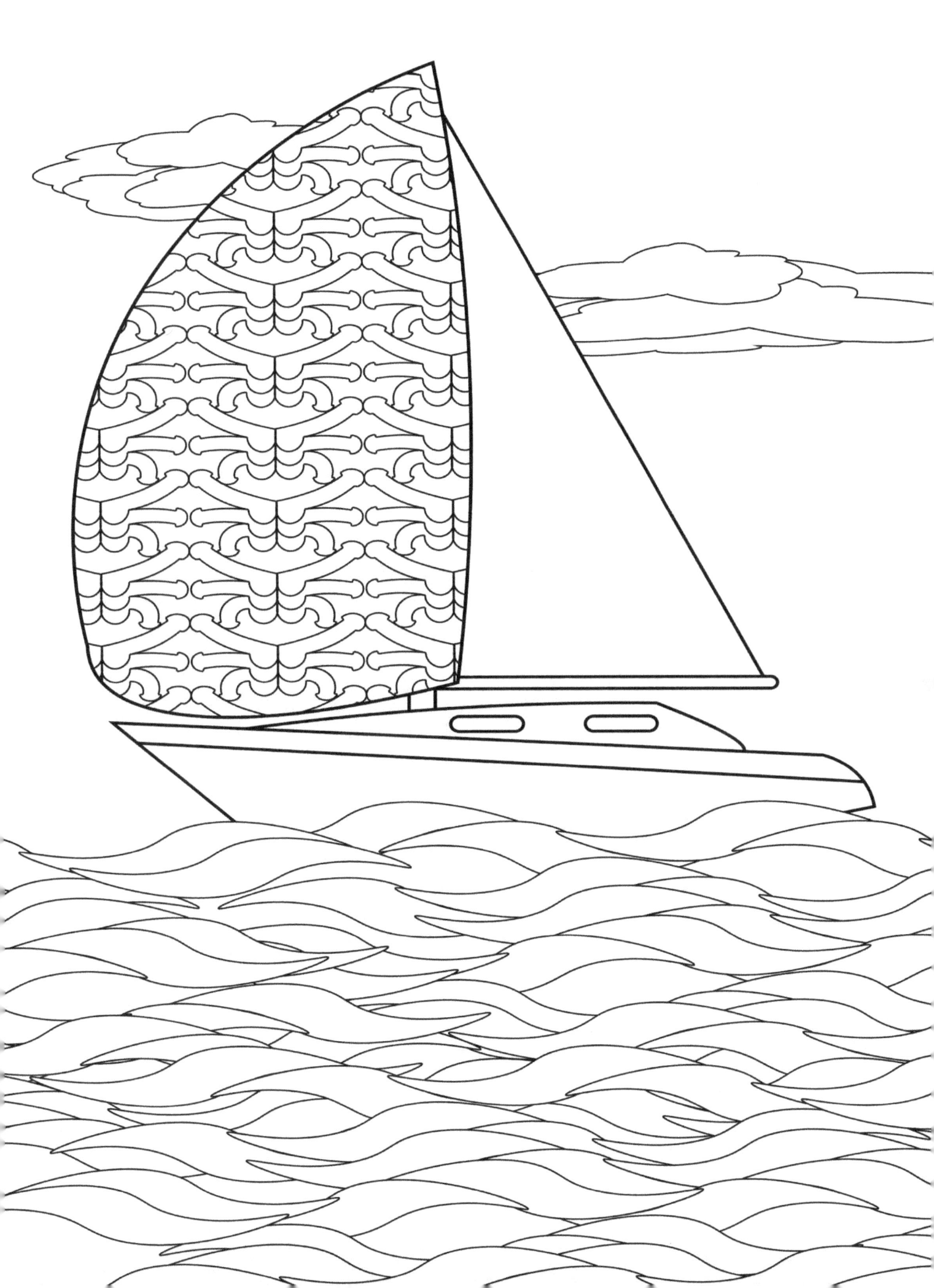

"Thanks for coming!"

- Receptionist at the Sperm Bank

On the next picture, if you get some scissors and trim out the the leaves at the bottom of the picture, the tree will look bigger.

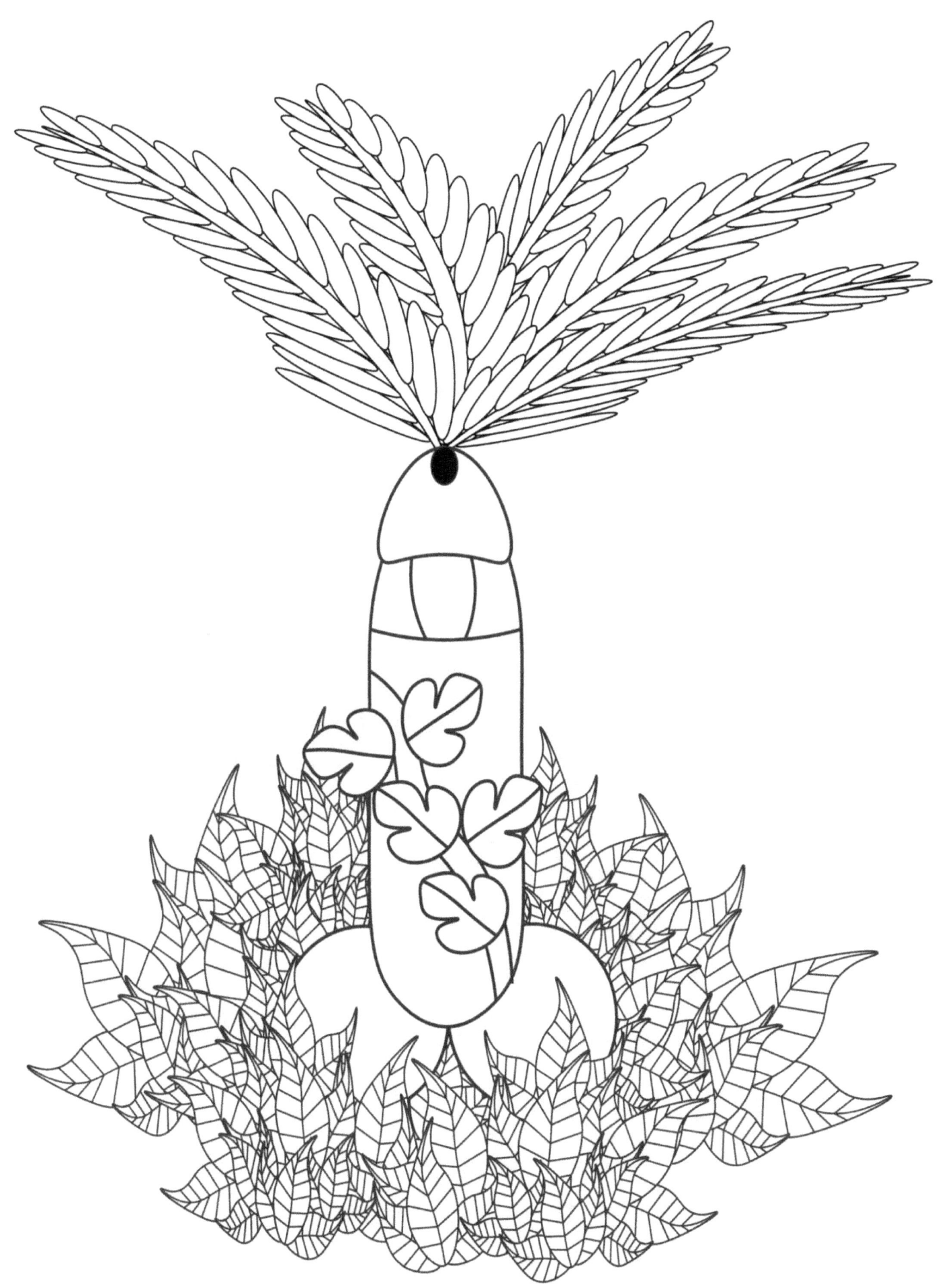

Father to his son: "You better stop masturbating or you'll go blind!"

Son: "Dad, I'm over here!"

Now, a completely non-sexual scene with a butterfly and flowers. If you see anything else, that's on you!

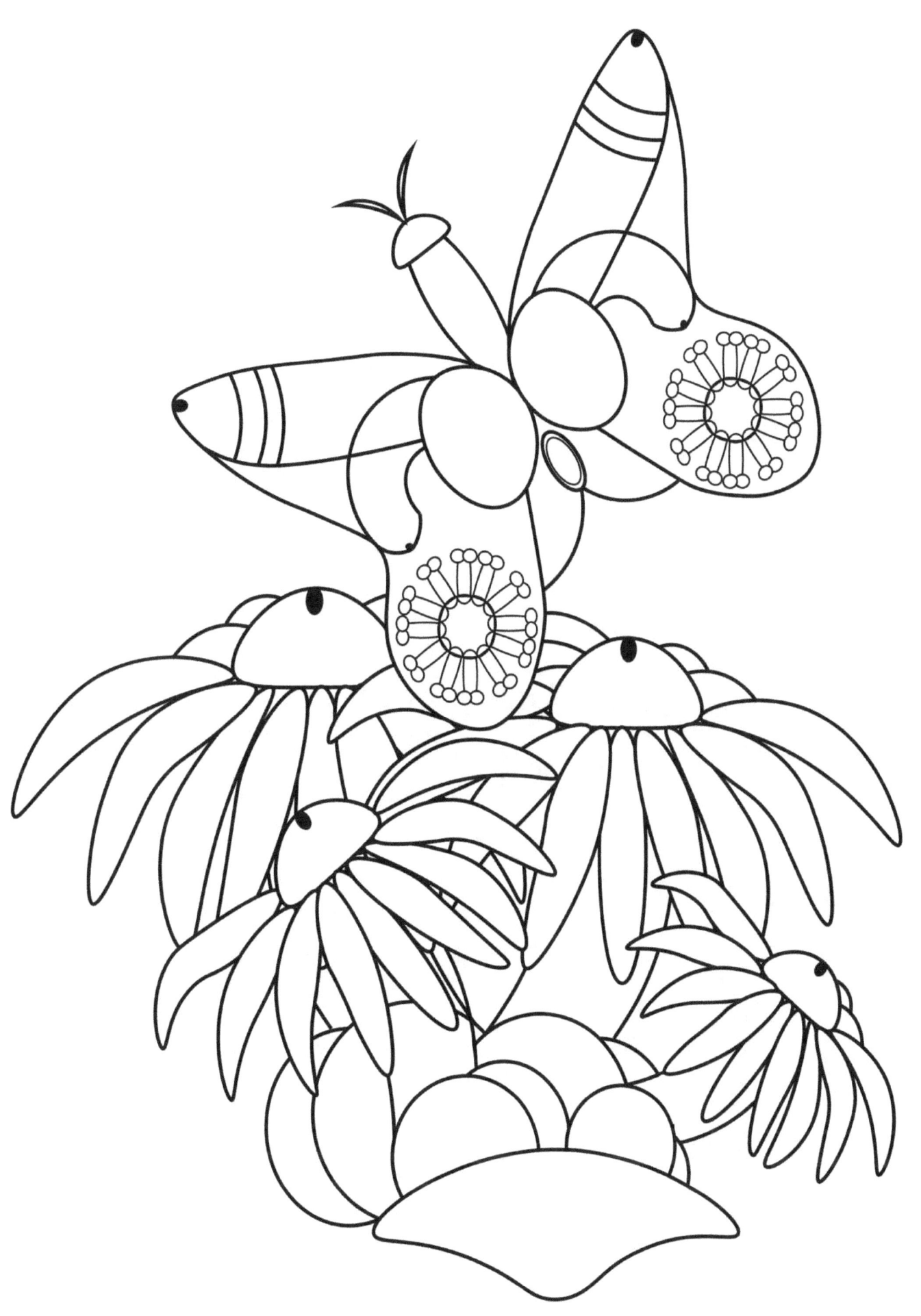

Man: "If I washed my cock, would you suck it?"

Woman: "No!!!"

Man: "You dirty cock-sucker!"

Our next coloring page is something completely different... No, not really, it's a stack of cocks within cocks! What did you expect from an adult coloring book called *Whimsical Willies*?

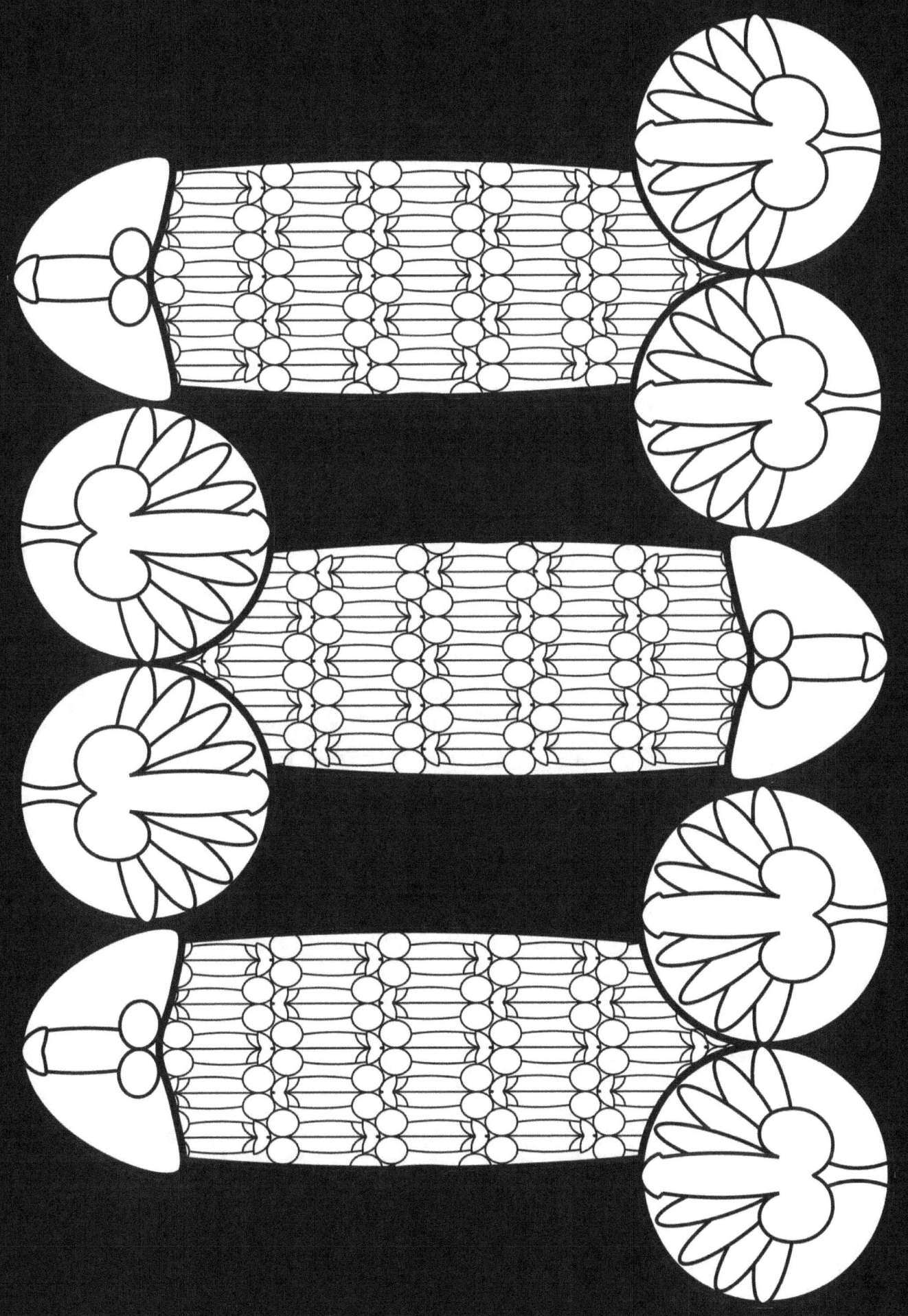

Two guys are at the urinals and one looks over and notices that the other has a nicotine patch on his penis. "I'm not a doctor or anything, but isn't that patch supposed to go on your arm?" he asks. The other guy shakes his head. "I don't know about that, but it's working fine – I'm down to two butts per day!"

Seems like it's time to give you another cock mandala to color. Yep... definitely time for that!

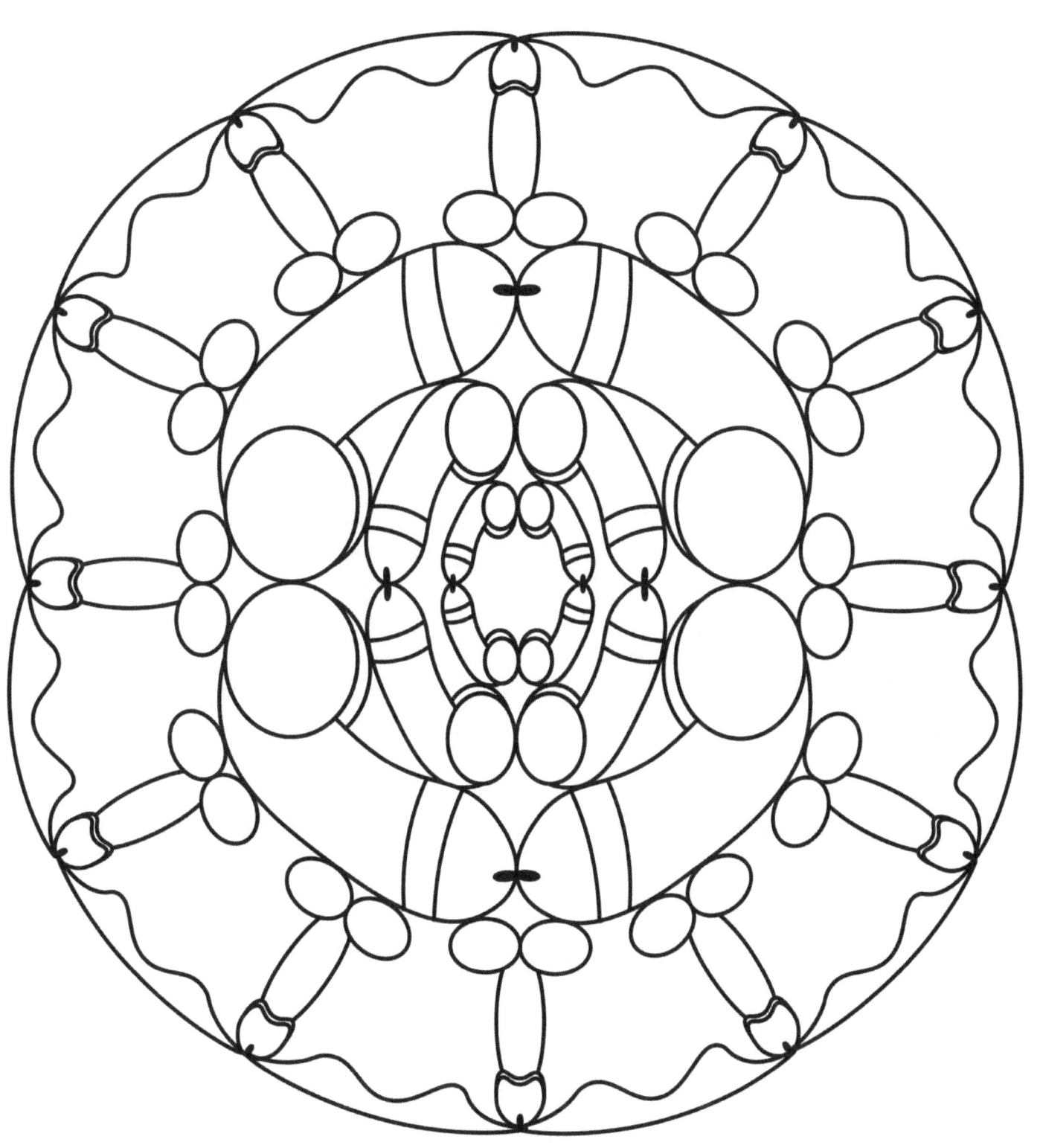

Three men make a bet as to who can make their wife scream more from sex. The next day, the three compare notes to see who won:

The first guy says, "I fucked my wife hard for almost 45 minutes straight and she was screaming her head off at least half that time!"

The second guy says, "That's nothing! I went down on my wife for over an hour and she screamed with every lick!

The third guy says, "I kicked both your asses on this one! Last night I fucked my wife for about two minutes before I came. Then I pulled out, got up, and wiped my cock off on the new curtains and she's still screaming!"

And now a majestic view of a hot air balloon. Definitely no dicks in this one! If you see any, it may be time to take a break from this coloring book – too many cocks have gone to your head!

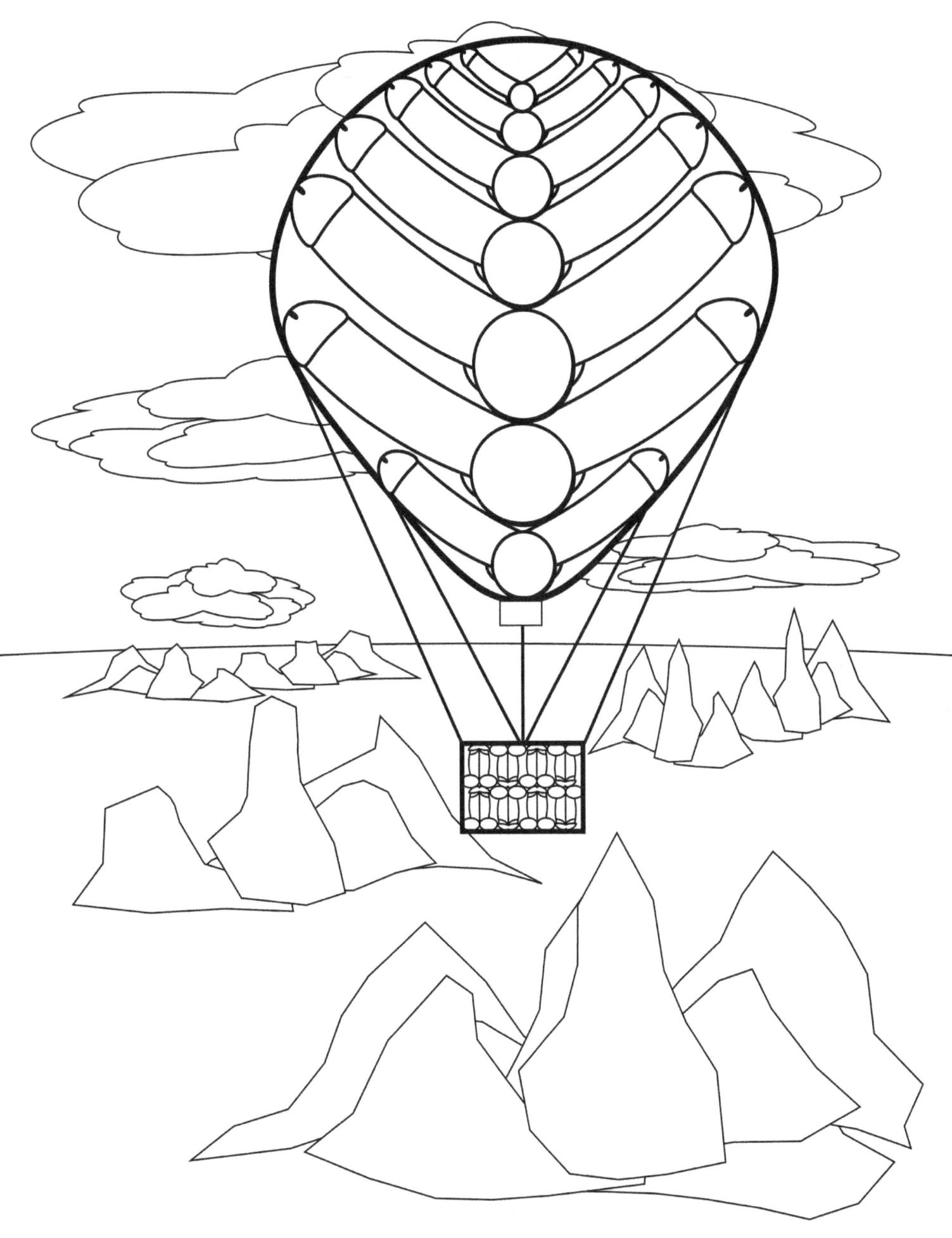

Tom is insecure about his "stamina" in bed, so he asks his friend Rick, who's a notorious ladies' man, for advice.

Rick tells him, "What I do before I'm about to have sex is slam my dick hard on the dresser so that it swells up and gets numb. That way, I'm bigger and last longer!"

Tom decides to try it that night. Entering the bedroom, he finds his wife already sound asleep in bed with the lights out. After stripping off his boxers and fumbling his way in the dark to the dresser, he takes a deep breath and slams his cock hard on top of it.

The noise stirs Tom's wife from her sleep and she groggily calls out from the bed, "Rick, is that you?"

Things can change in a hurry in this funny, dirty coloring book! The next picture kind of reminds me of the movie, *Predator* for some reason.

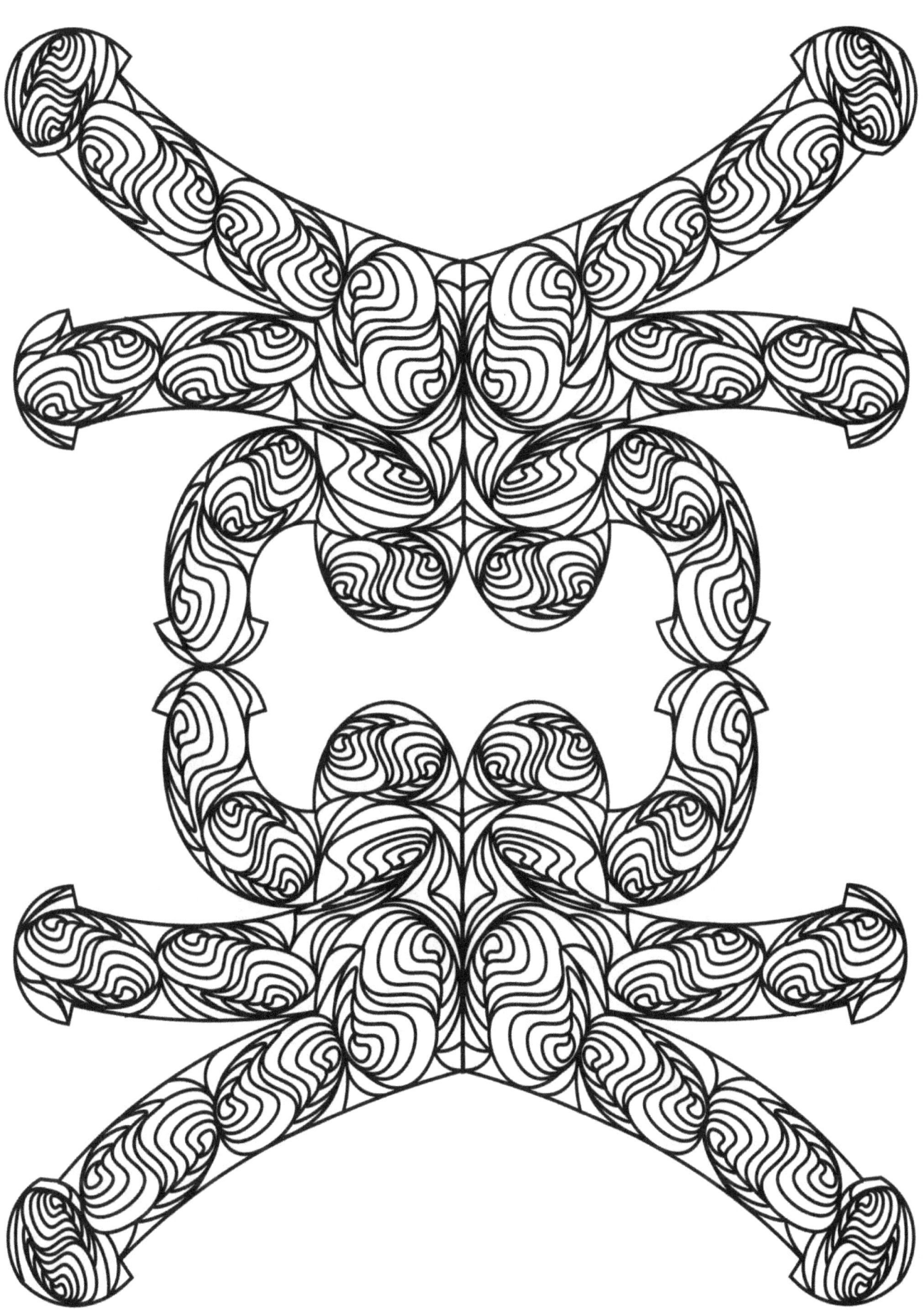

A penis has a tough life. His hair is a mess, his family is nuts, his neighbor is an asshole, his best friend is a pussy, and he's frequently beaten by his owner!

Let's switch things up a bit with a lovely floral arrangement for you to color!

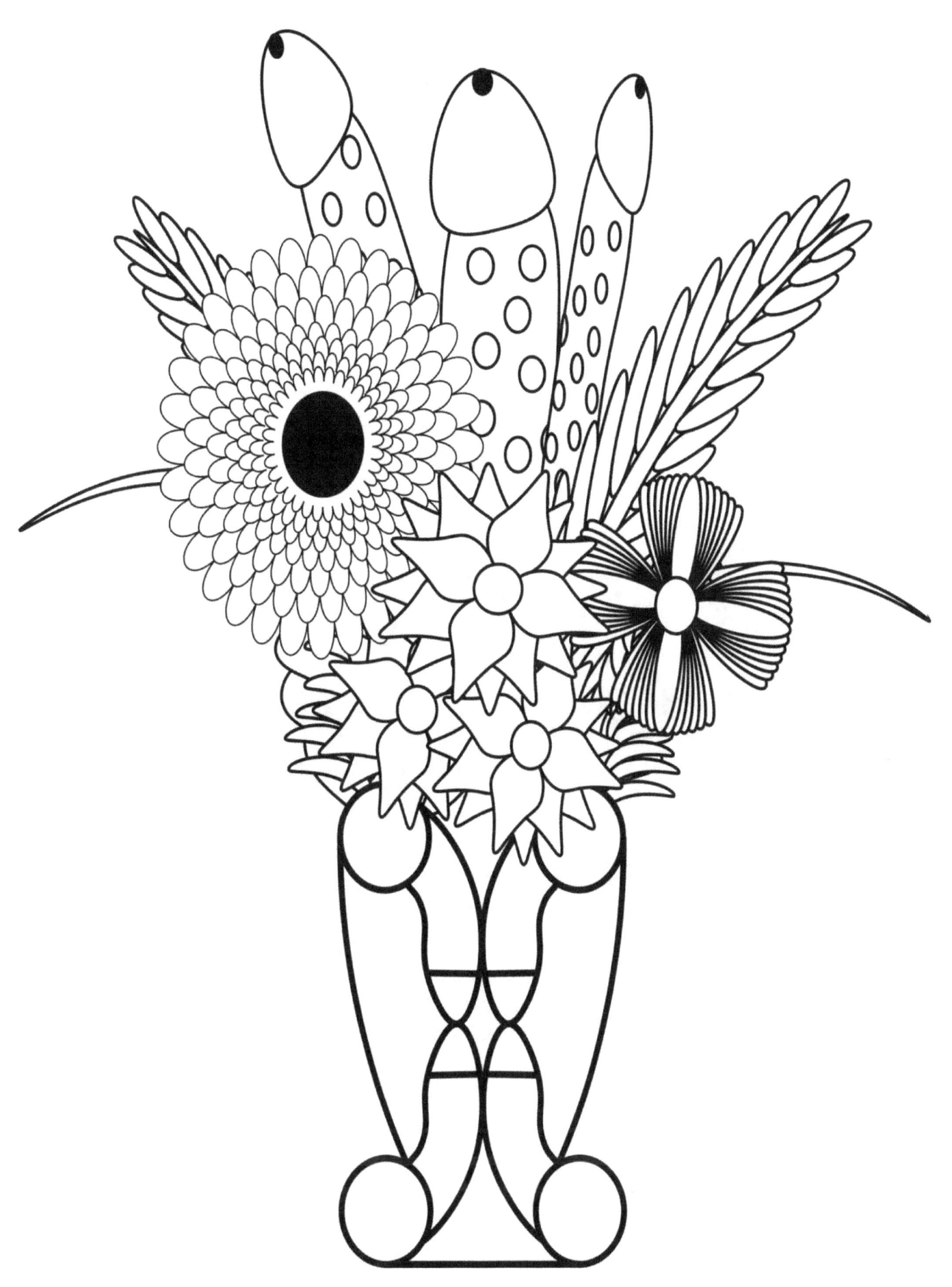

A man is so crazy in love with his girlfriend, Wendy, he gets her name tattooed on his cock. One day he's at the urinals in a public restroom and notices the dreadlocked man next to him also has "Wendy" tattooed on his dick. "Excuse me, I couldn't help but notice your tattoo since I have the same thing. Is Wendy the name of your wife? Girlfriend?"

The dreadlocked man looks at him quizzically for a moment before suddenly getting a broad grin on his face. In a Caribbean accent he replies, "Oh, no mon! My tattoo not say 'Wendy'. When I get hard, you see, it say, 'Welcome to Jamaica and have a nice day,' mon!"

While most of the pictures in this adult coloring book have been pretty fanciful, the next page includes at least a bit of realism. The phallic flowers are Mexican hat coneflowers, a common variety of wildflower native to most of North America.

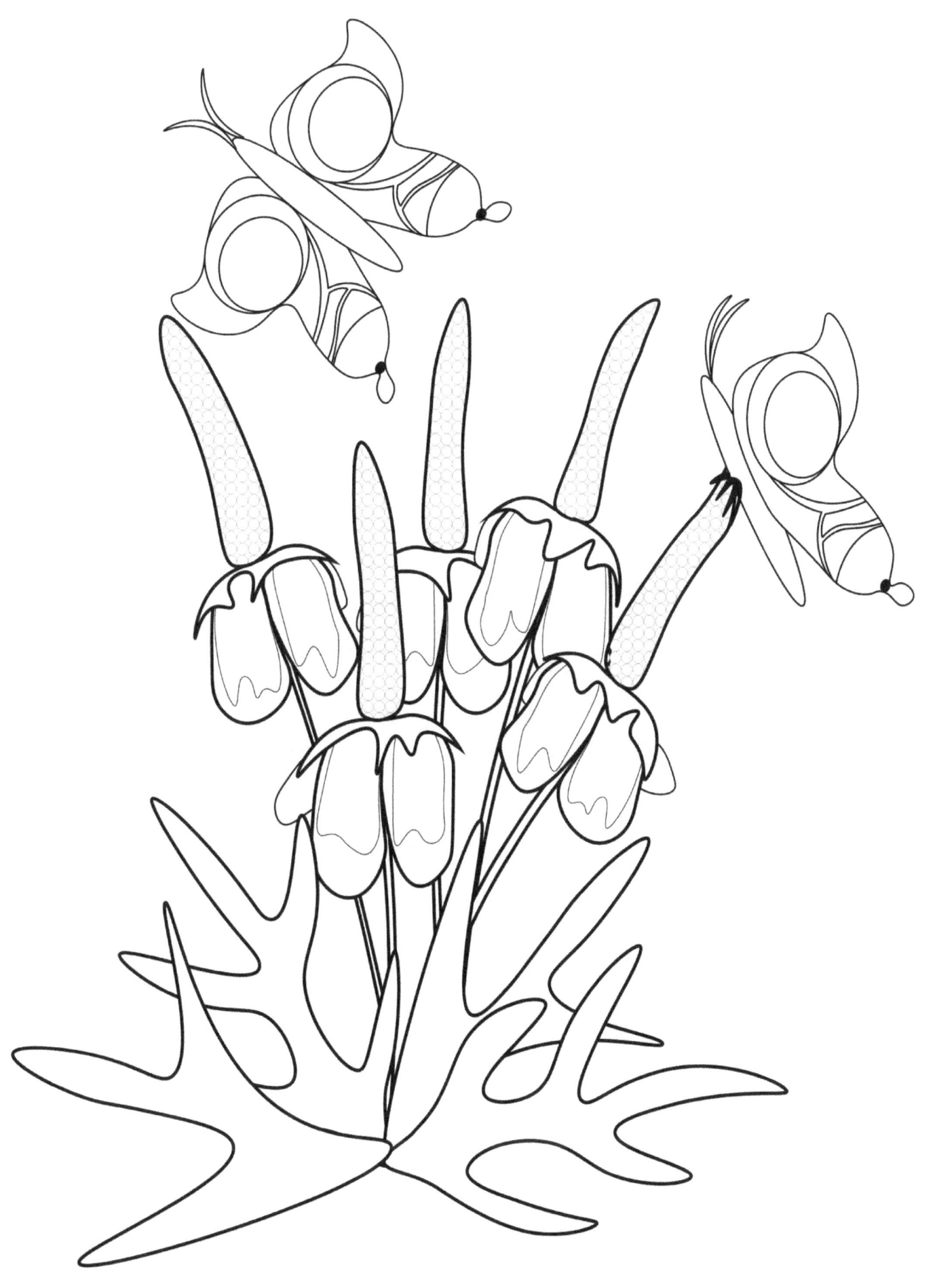

Posted to a Sex Q&A Forum -
Q:"What is a penis supposed to smell like? My brother-in-law's penis smells like meatloaf. Is that normal?
A: "That you know what your brother-in-law's penis smells like? No! That's definitely not normal!"

We've had a number of sexual mandalas in this very "adult" coloring book already, so now I bring you the multi-mandala – on a sexy black background!

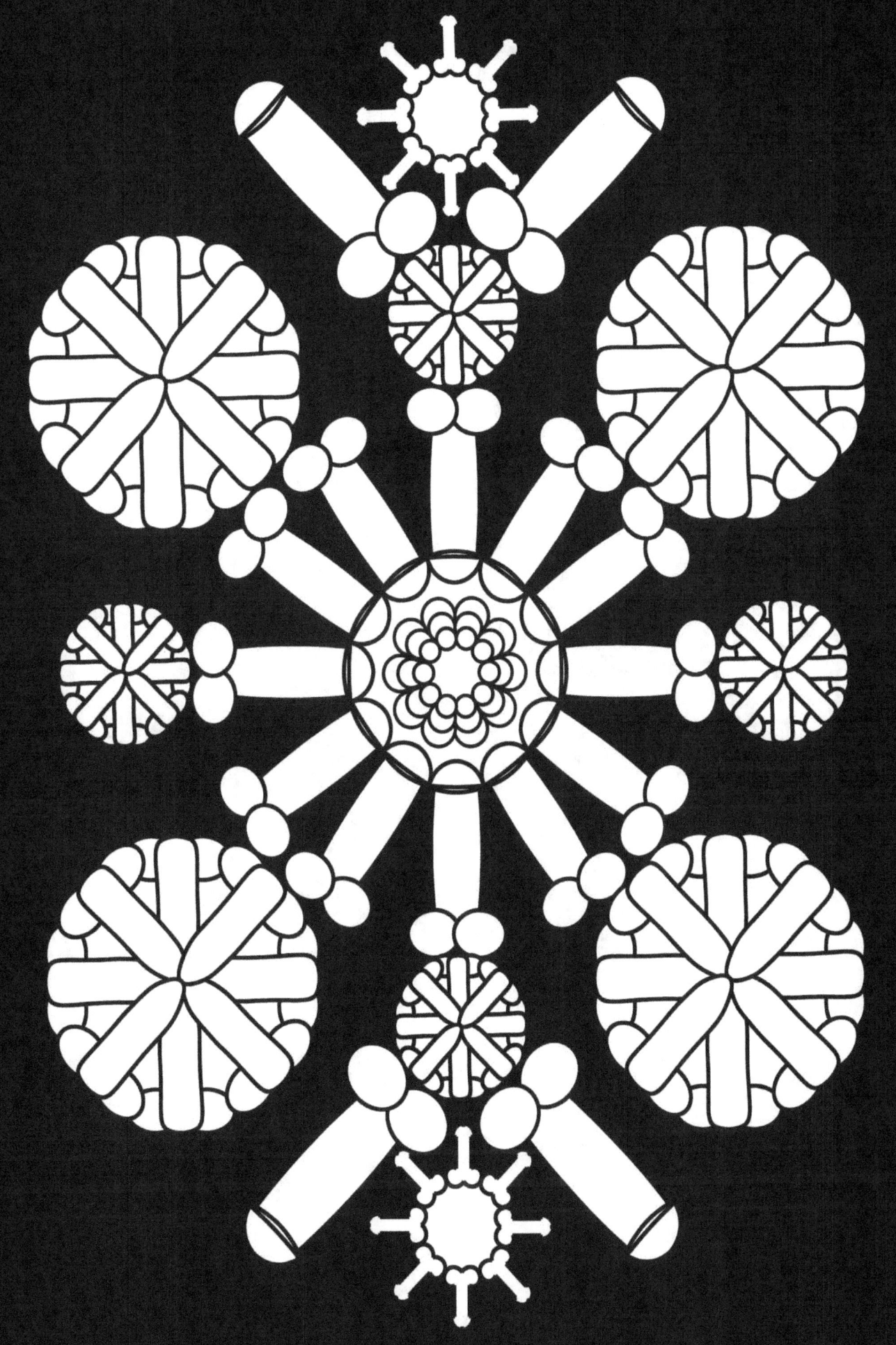

Two women go to the movies. After taking their seats, a man sits down by himself next to them. Halfway through the movie, the woman closest to the man leans over and whispers to her friend, "You're not going to believe this, but the guy next to me just shoved a hand down the front of his pants!"

"Ugh! Well, I'm really into the movie. Can you maybe just ignore him?" her friend whispers back.

"I would, but it's MY hand!"

Need more anger-management or stress-relief from your coloring? How about a nice, relaxing beach scene – just be careful not to get crabs!

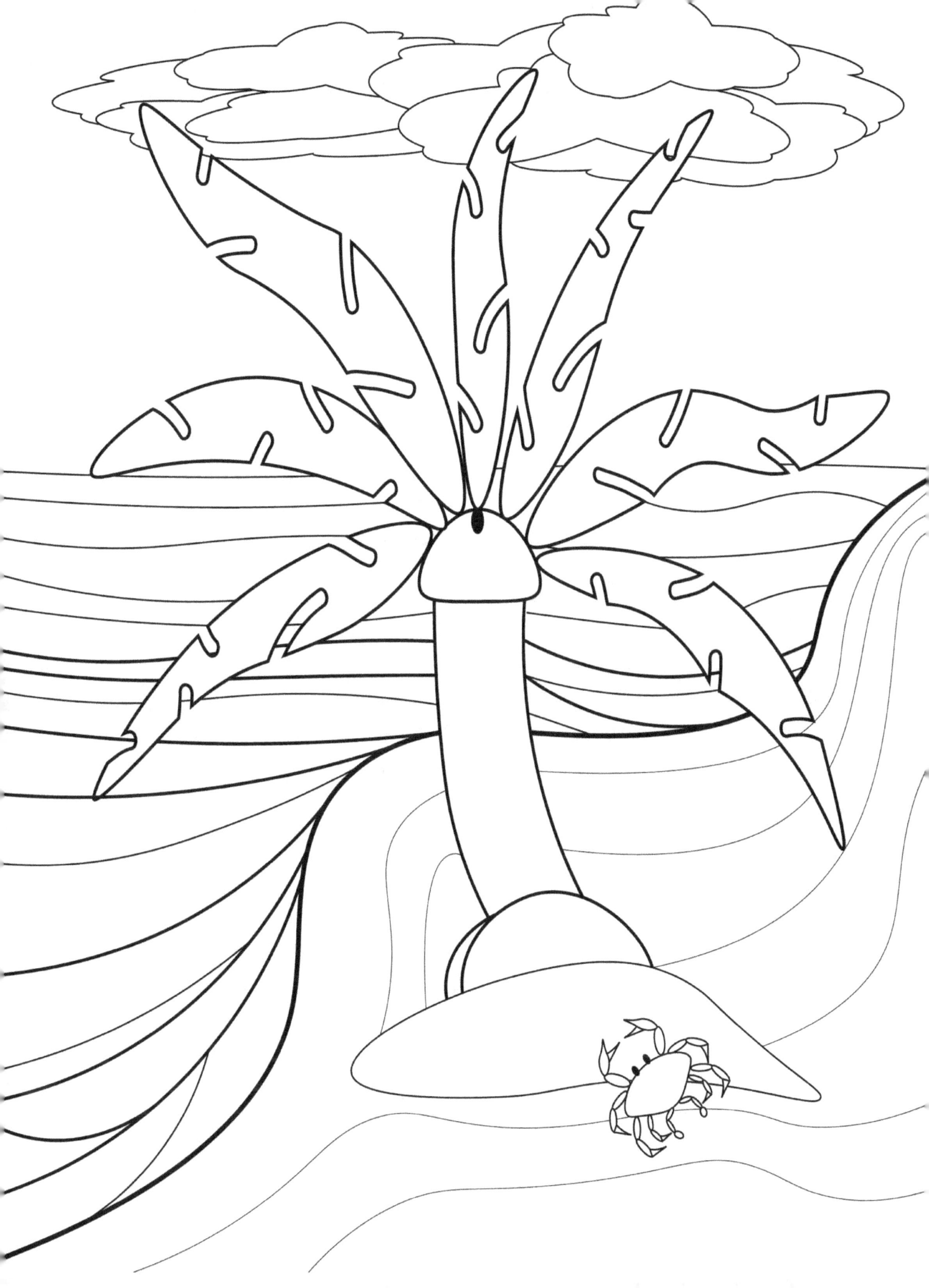

"Instead of my little bottle of energy drink, I accidentally took a swig from a bottle of White Out last night. I woke up this morning with a massive correction!"

- Anonymous

One more butterfly and flower picture for you to apply your mad coloring skills to. Once again, just a nice, pretty picture without any cocks in it at all. Nope, not a one!

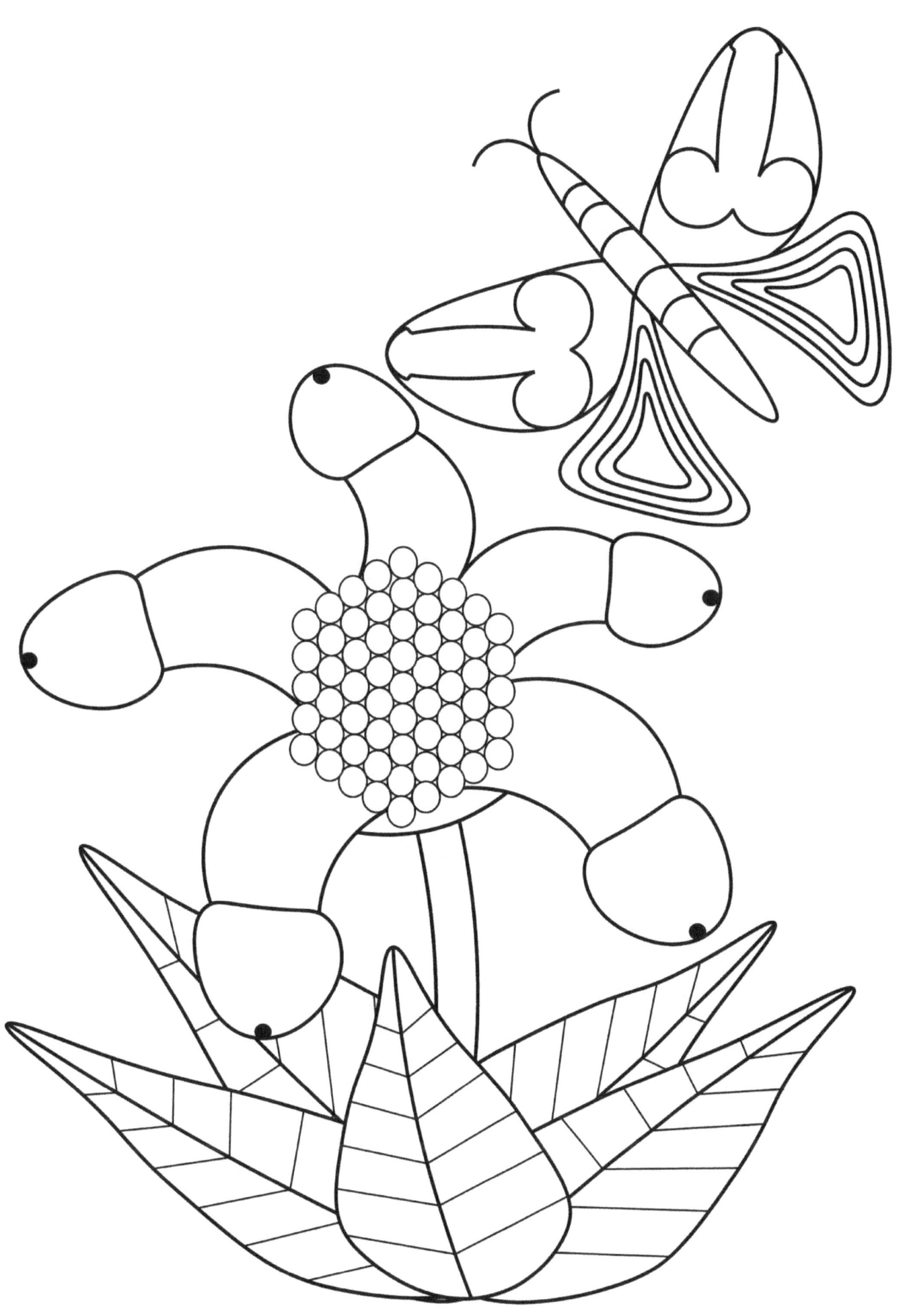

"Two facts about me:
1) My penis is not as long as a foot-long sub sandwich.
2) I am banned for life from the sub shop where I determined fact #1."

- Anonymous (Except at the sub shop, where they definitely know his name!)

The next page is an intricate coloring pattern that's a veritable cornucopia of cock!

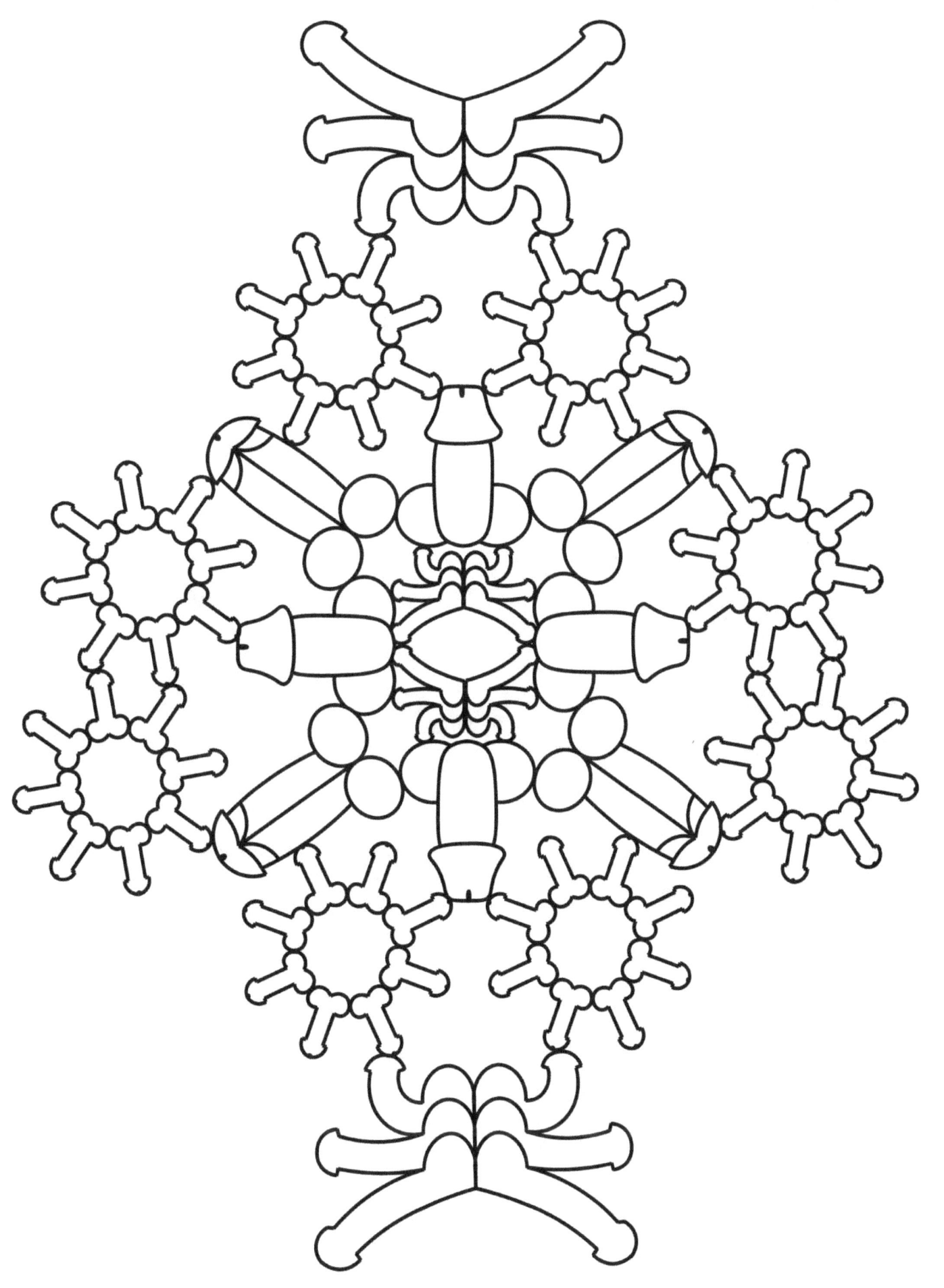

The teacher walked into the classroom to find the word "penis" chalked in small letters on the board. She was a bit embarrassed, so she didn't say anything, but rubbed it out and went on with the class.

But the next day when she came in, she found the same thing again - "penis", this time written slightly larger. So she rubbed it out again, and went on with the lesson.

Again next day, in even larger letters, there was the word "penis" again. With a red face she rubbed it out and went on with the lesson.

Well, this went on for a whole week, every day the word penis getting bigger.

Finally, on Friday she went into the classroom to find chalked up: "See, the more you rub it, the bigger it gets!"

Maybe it's the star patterns, or perhaps the explosion, but the next adults only coloring page makes me think of the Fourth of July.

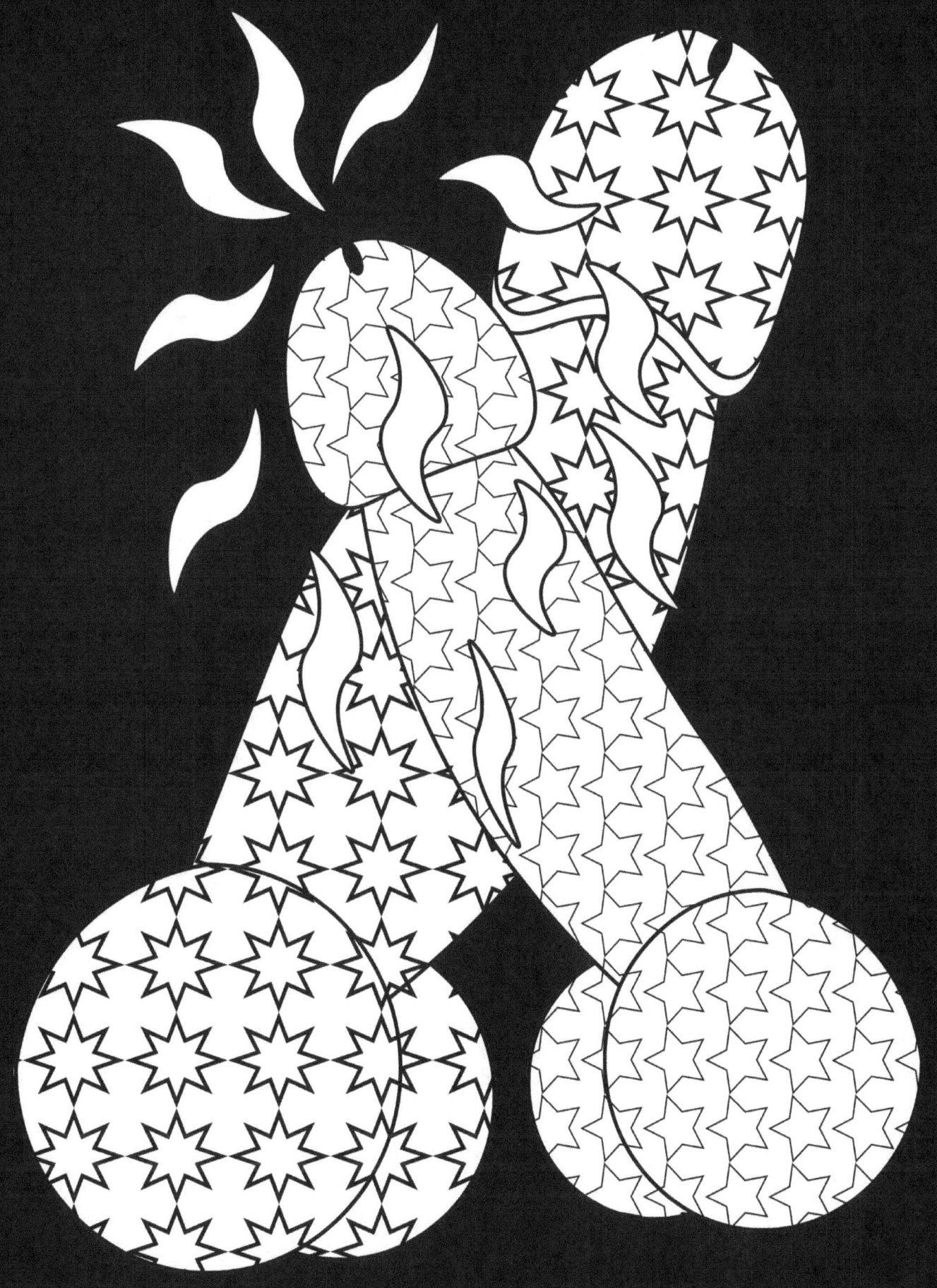

Why did the pervert cross the road?
His dick was stuck in the chicken!

Our next stress-relief coloring book entry is a gentle reminder that sometimes you need to slow down a little.

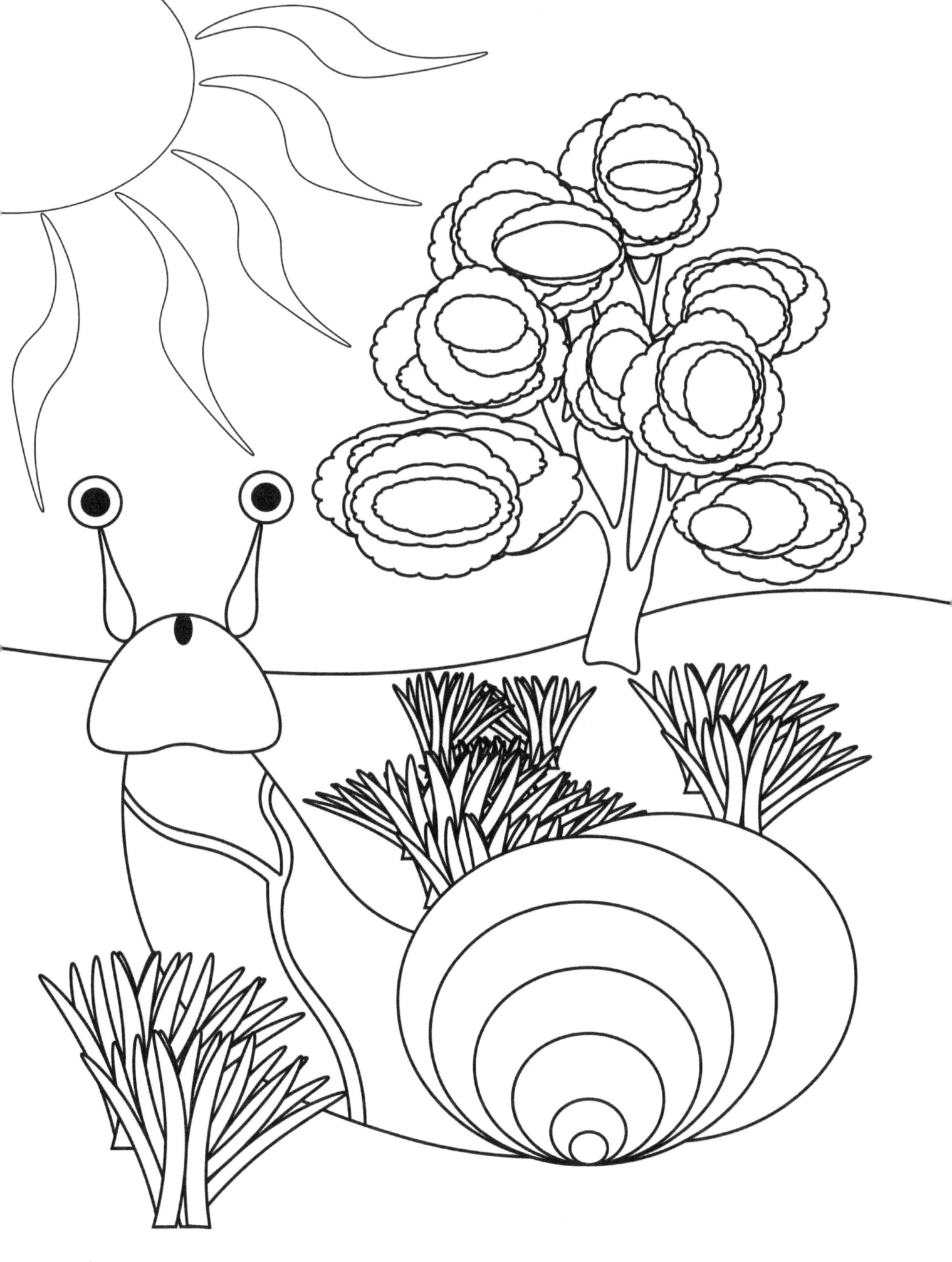

"Herpes is a strong word. I prefer the term 'genital sprinkles'."

- Anonymous, But Very Possibly Someone You've Slept With!

And speaking of spotted dicks, if you've ever played with a Light Brite, the next picture will probably seem familiar.

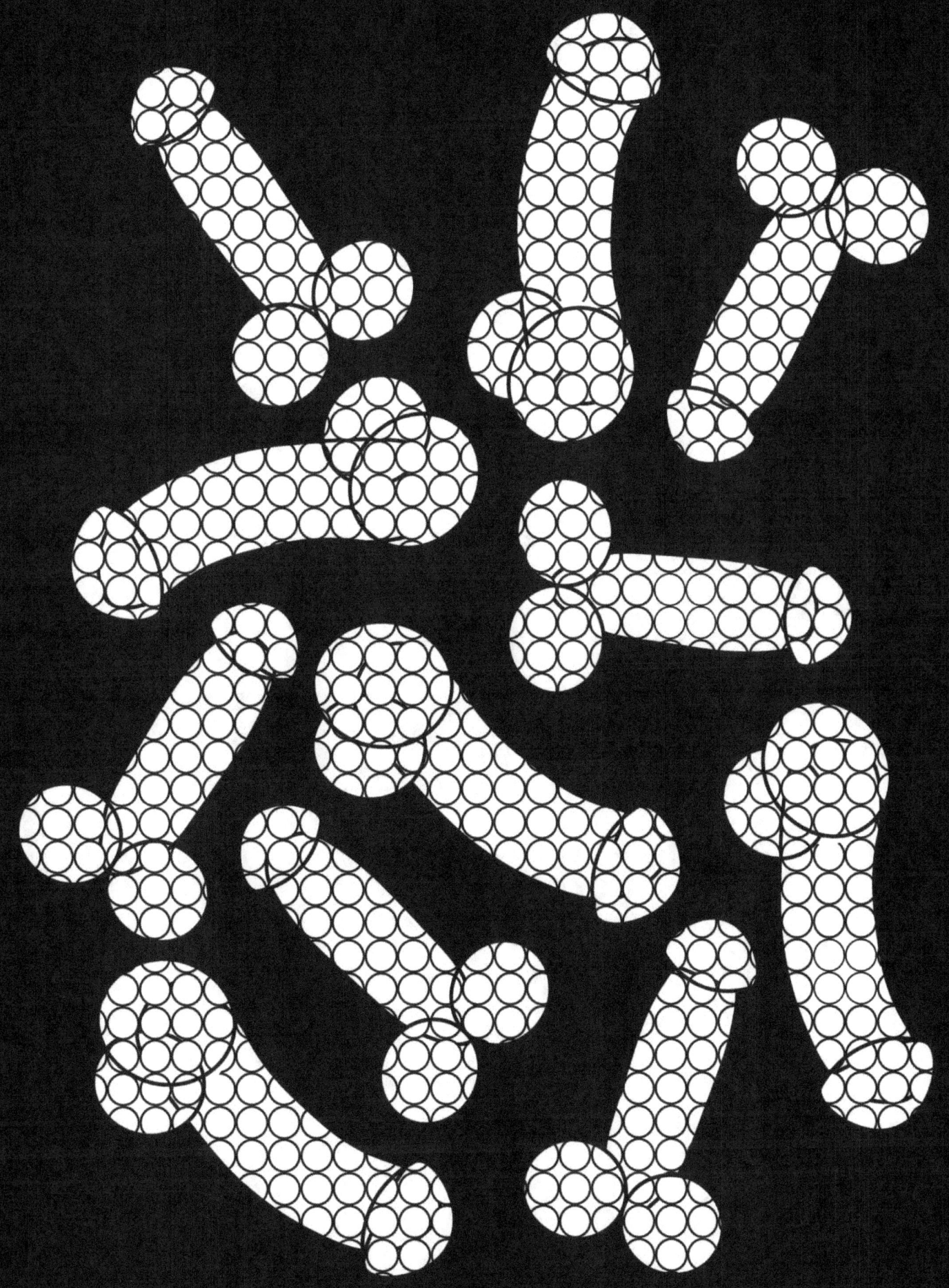

One sperm asks the other "how far until we get to the ovaries?" "We've still got a long way to go," the second sperm said. "We just passed the tonsils."

Shall we have another multi-dick geometric pattern in this risqué adult coloring book? Yes, I think we shall!

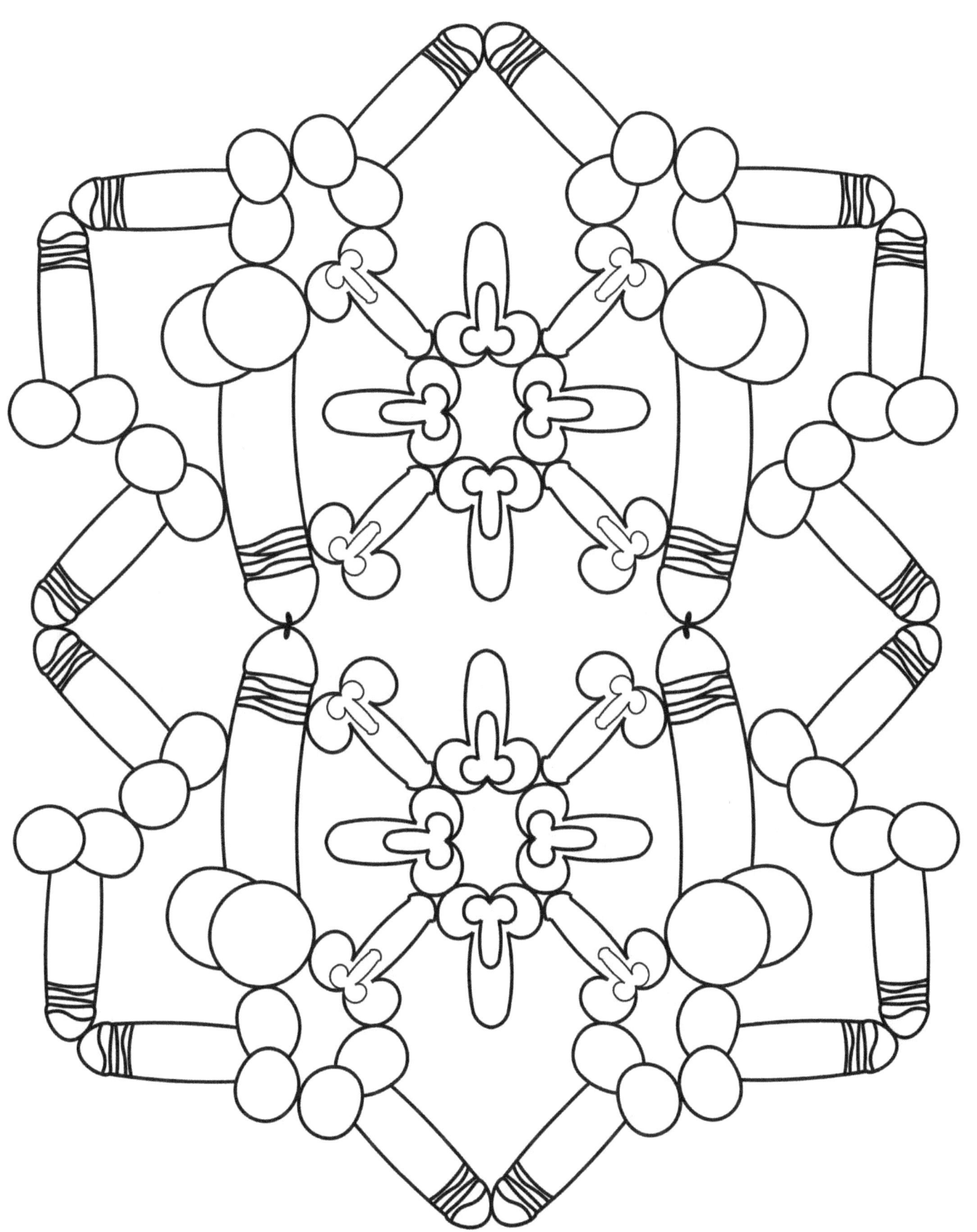

A chicken farmer went to a local bar, sat next to a woman and ordered a glass of champagne. The woman looks up and says "How about that? I just ordered a glass of champagne, too!"

"What a coincidence," the farmer says. "This is a special day for me .. I am celebrating."

"This is a special day for me too, I am also celebrating!" says the woman.

"What a coincidence!" says the farmer. As they clinked glasses the man asked "What are you celebrating?"

"My husband and I have been trying to have a child and today my gynecologist told me that I am pregnant!"

"What a coincidence," says the man. "I'm a chicken farmer and for months many of my hens were infertile, but today they are all laying fertilized eggs!" "That's great!" says the woman, "How did your chickens become fertile?"

"I used a different cock," he replied.

The woman smiled and said, "What a coincidence!"

All good things come to an end, but there's one last picture of two fancy cocks to round out this naughty coloring book.

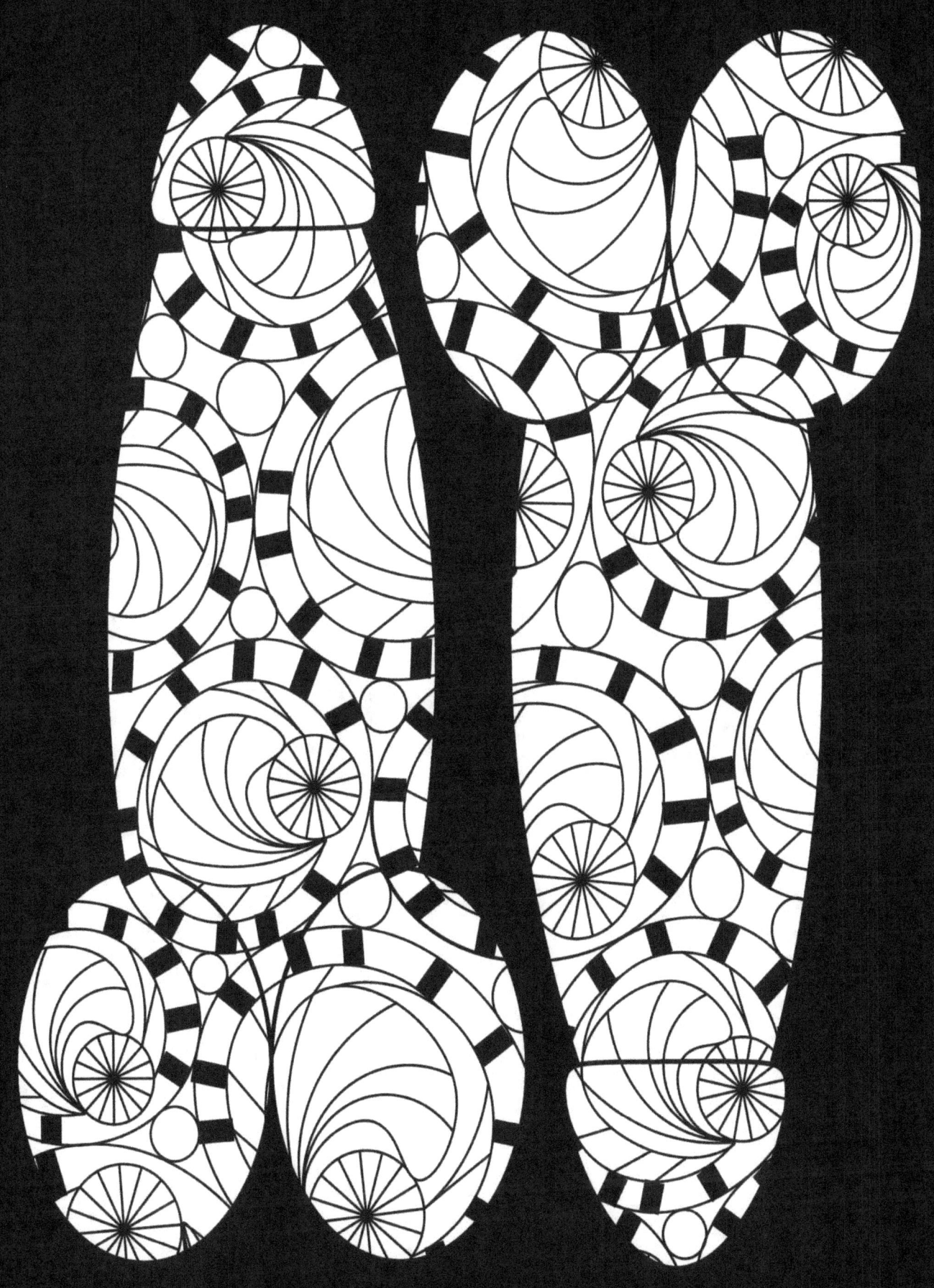

We hope you've enjoyed
Whimsical Willies: The Adults-Only Funny & Naughty Cock Coloring Book!

If you have comments, questions, and/or requests for content in future adult coloring or game books, or if you would like to join our email list to receive notices of new products and exclusive FREE subscriber-only coloring pages and other content, please visit us at:

Nawteefun.com